VIRGIN DAD

THE FIRST-TIME DAD'S ESSENTIAL GUIDE TO
PREGNANCY: HOW TO SUPPORT YOUR PARTNER,
REDUCE SELF-DOUBT, AND BE A DAD WHO PROVIDES

THE HANDBOOK

JESSE HAYES

CONTENTS

Introduction   7

1. YOU'RE LATE THIS MONTH?—THE
   FIRST MONTH   13
   Week One: Not Official Yet   13
   Week Two: In Anticipation of Ovulation   16
   Week Three: The Perfectly Imperfect
   Conception   20
   Week Four: When in Doubt, Take a Test   22
   ☆ *A Personal Story*   26
   Questions and Answers: What Fathers
   Need to Know   30

2. LET ME HOLD YOUR HAIR BACK—THE
   SECOND MONTH   33
   Week Five: Evolution Now!   33
   Week Six   40
   Week Seven   45
   Week Eight   54
   ☆ *A Personal Story*   71
   Questions and Answers: What Fathers
   Need to Know   75

3. LOVELY BABY BUMPS —THE THIRD
   MONTH   79
   Week Nine   79
   Week Ten   84
   Week Eleven   90
   Week Twelve: The End of the First
   Trimester   94
   Ways to Make Your Partner Feel Secure   98
   Saving for Labor Day and Beyond   104

Red Flags During First Trimester 114
☆ *Home Is Where the Heart Beats: A Personal Story* 116
Questions and Answers: What Fathers Need to Know 119

4. DID YOU SAY YOU'RE HORNY?—THE FOURTH MONTH 123
Week Thirteen 124
Week Fourteen 129
Week Fifteen 133
Week Sixteen 139
Announcing Your Pregnancy 142
Take Her Clothes Shopping 145
☆ *Tummy Tum-Tum: A Personal Story* 147
Questions and Answers: What Fathers Need to Know 151

5. NUTS OR NO NUTS? - GENDER REVEAL TIME—THE FIFTH MONTH 153
Week Seventeen 153
Week Eighteen 156
Week Nineteen 158
Week Twenty 161
The Great "Revealing" Ultrasound 163
Documenting the Journey 165
Mom is Catching the Sniffles Much More 166
Ready for a Babymoon? 168
Questions and Answers: What Fathers Need to Know 169

6. I FELT THE KICK!—THE SIXTH MONTH 171
Week Twenty-One 171
Week Twenty-Two 175
Week Twenty-Three 178
Week Twenty-Four 181
Preparing For the Glucose Test 183

Organizing the Baby Registry 184
Signs of Preterm Labor 185
☆ *Don't Drink the Kool-Aid: A Personal Story* 187
Questions and Answers: What Fathers Need to Know 190

7. PEDIATRICIAN? THE BABY ISN'T EVEN HERE YET!—THE SEVENTH MONTH 193
Week Twenty-Five 193
Week Twenty-Six 196
Week Twenty-Seven: Leaving the Second Trimester 198
Week Twenty-Eight: Enter the Third Trimester 201
Choosing a Baby Name 203
Missing Your Old Life? 206
Knowing the Signs of Preeclampsia 207
Finding a Pediatrician 208
☆ *Dog-Lover Like Daddy: A Personal Story* 211
Questions and Answers: What Fathers Need to Know 213

8. WADDLE BABY WADDLE BABY—THE EIGHTH MONTH 215
Week Twenty-Nine 215
Week Thirty 218
Week Thirty-One 220
Week Thirty-Two 222
The Baby Shower 224
Stock Up on Essentials 225
The Pregnancy Waddle 226

9. TICKING TIME MOM 229
Week Thirty-Three 229
Week Thirty-Four 232
Week Thirty-Five 234
Week Thirty-Six 236

What Is Breech? 238

The Discussion: Breast Versus Bottle 239

Make Freezer Meals for Post-Delivery 240

☆ *You Have to Know Love to Show Love: A Personal Story* 242

Questions and Answers: What Fathers Need to Know 243

10. YES, SHE'S STILL PREGNANT 245

Week Thirty-Seven 246

Week Thirty-Eight 247

Week Thirty-Nine 249

Week Forty 251

What Happens if the Baby Is Past Due? 253

What to Know About Being Induced 255

What to Expect During Birth 256

What if She Has a C-Section? 258

☆ *Let's Just Have Sex, Already: A Personal Story* 259

Questions and Answers: What Fathers Need to Know 261

11. CALL ME "DADDY"—THE FIRST 11 MONTHS WITH A BABY 263

The First Month 263

The Second Month 265

The Third Month 268

Reconnecting With Your Spouse 269

☆ *Starting Back at One: A Personal Story* 272

Questions and Answers: What Fathers Need to Know 274

Conclusion 277

References 283

INTRODUCTION

When you're young, you think your dad is Superman. Then you grow up and realize he's just a regular guy who wears a cape.

— DAVE ATELL

"I am pregnant." These three words can change your life forever. Being a father is an honorable duty, especially when you're fortunate enough to experience your child's entire growth period. It's like watching a whole other human being formed from nothing into something.

It's truly a turning point in the life of any man who understands the responsibility that comes with not only fathering a child but being around to actively raise one. But before enjoying the spoils of your and your wife's labor (no pun intended), the first hurdle to cross together will be the 40 weeks of development—from an embryo to a full-term newborn. This is the most crucial time as you will need to be emotionally, psychologically, physically, and financially prepared to support your wife and your growing baby.

This is where *Virgin Dad: The First-Time Dad's Essential Guide to Pregnancy: How to Support Your Partner, Reduce Self-Doubt, and Be a Dad Who Provides – The Handbook* comes in as a guide to take you through each phase of pregnancy incrementally, preparing you for what to expect and how to react to ensure the best care and support are given to your partner as well as the safe delivery of your bundle of joy. Undoubtedly, it's an exciting time for both of you. I mean, you're about to share in the creation of an entirely new being, a perfect blend of your respective DNA—exciting is a bit of an understatement! Now that you're aware of your pivotal role in being a strong support to your pregnant spouse as well as the duties of a dad (which have already begun), in what ways will you take charge of this situation? More importantly, what are you supposed to do during the birthing process? Hollywood shows us depictions of overwhelmed men collapsing at the hospital bedside, unable to stomach the sight of natural birth. These are precisely the sorts of situations you should be prepared to endure. You don't want to be the guy who's so overrun with anxiety that he allows palpitations and shock to rob him of one of the most memorable times in his life while neglecting to be a strong support for his wife.

There is no need to worry if you think you fall into this category. This book has everything imaginable that you need to know, and even some things you'll wish you didn't know, so consider yourself warned! The dynamic of roles between a man and a woman, though natural, can be profound and complex, especially when the topic of pregnancy is involved. You will need to navigate through her shifting moods, accommodate her sporadic cravings and changes in appetite, anticipate her fatigue and sickness, and several other awkward situations. This book is full of nuggets that will save you the headache of trying to "figure it out" in the moment. The best advice you can hope to find is from someone who has lived through the experience. And having supported my wife through multiple pregnancies, I understand exactly what you're going through. Having such a great weight of responsibility can be intimidating, even to a self-declared veteran like myself. My aim with this book is to give every soon-to-be father the tools and knowledge needed to handle this pregnancy like a champ—even if you are a virgin dad!

In my opinion, there is not enough sound advice from personal experience for men when it comes to maneuvering the complexities of pregnancy. It takes a great deal of mental strength, courage, and commitment to maintain a balanced emotional presence for yourself, your partner, and the coming addition to your new family, while simultaneously preparing mentally to be a full-time parent. Believe me, it helps to know what should be done ahead of time in a situation as sensitive as pregnancy, and luckily, you have me here to lend my wisdom. They say ignorance is bliss, but being ignorant of how to effectively handle your partner's pregnancy can have serious and even irreversible effects. Remember that everything Mama eats, the baby eats. Similarly, everything mama feels, the baby also feels. Being informed of what foods are most nutritious for your partner and the development of the baby is key to keeping them both safe throughout the pregnancy and until delivery.

The most important "P's" a man has to live by are these: to procreate, to provide, and to protect. The procreation part can be lots of fun, but it comes with a great deal of responsibility. This is where the other two P's come into the equation. Although life is different in our modern society where women go out to work and can earn a living for themselves, it remains the duty of a man to first provide financial stability and then emotional stability, which both bring a level of security and protection.

It was the famous actor Matthew McConaughey who said, "They eat, they crap, they sleep. And if they're crying, they need to do one of the three, and they're having trouble doing it. Real simple." Sure, that may be an oversimplification of the entirety of a father's bucket list of duties, but it makes for a decent illustration of what the role entails for both the child and your spouse. I am not implying that your wife is a child, but ensuring that she eats and sleeps well and that her all-around health is intact is paramount, especially during pregnancy.

It's a habit of dads to worry about things, being the perpetual problem solvers that we are. But despite the anxiety and uncertainty that accompany the entire process of pregnancy, from implantation to conception, the best thing to do for yourself, your spouse, and the growing baby is to be present physically and emotionally. It's easy to shut down under the weight of all the pressure, but once you prepare the basics beforehand, the rest of your time and effort should be to support your spouse. Remember that it's a foreign experience for her too if it's your first child together. So, being that solid rock of support throughout every step of your partner's pregnancy will be a priceless gift she will forever cherish and love you for. Be encouraged, because in the end, your sacrifices for her and the baby will all be worth it.

1

YOU'RE LATE THIS MONTH?— THE FIRST MONTH

WEEK ONE: NOT OFFICIAL YET

Expecting a baby is just the beginning. There are so many precious moments to look forward to as your baby grows. These moments can start with something as simple as, "Honey…, I'm late this month." Hearing this after months of a normal cycle can leave a man lost for words. Your immediate reaction may be to respond with questions that avert the possibility of the obvious, like:

- Are you sure it's late?
- Maybe you checked too early?
- Don't you think it's that new fasting method you've been on?

- How are you so sure it isn't something you ate?

But before the denial kicks in, the first week of pregnancy isn't exactly as obvious as one might hope to believe. In fact, the first week of pregnancy isn't a dead giveaway because the symptoms appear no different from those of your partner's regular menstrual cycle. If she suspects something and goes for a checkup, most obstetricians will only begin counting the days of pregnancy from the first day of your most recent period. Since a woman is most fertile during the time of ovulation and menstruation, it's more difficult to identify whether it's an actual conception or merely the completion of her cycle.

Simply put, the first week of pregnancy is regarded as a gray area, and the doctor may not declare your partner pregnant yet. As long as there are still physical signs of menstruation, the diagnosis remains in limbo. Depending on the length of her cycle, which typically runs about 28 days, after this time is when the baby is conceived, and all doubts can be laid to rest (The Bump, 2016).

When most couples discover they're expecting a baby, it's usually the fourth week already! Time flies when you're having fun. Remember, the first week of pregnancy mimics your partner's symptoms during her period cycle. Your spouse may already be familiar with a few of these symptoms and probably won't lose sleep over them. And you shouldn't either! But it's good to observe and know these signs for yourself so that you'll be able to pinpoint the cause of her mood swings and physical reactions for the next time you plan to have a baby! Knowledge is power. Here are her most common period symptoms:

- vaginal bleeding
- lower back pain
- bloating
- mood Swings
- headache

If either of you suspect the possibility of pregnancy based on the time in which you last had sex, be sure to discontinue any habits of your own that may be harmful to your partner and the unborn child, like smoking. Also, you may want to stop your partner from any form of alcohol consumption as well as from drinking more than two cups of coffee per day. Prepare meals that are high in vitamins and minerals, especially iron and folic acid. The latter can be found in any over-the-counter prenatal vitamin.

Remember, while this is likely her first week of pregnancy, all these are indicative of her body's monthly process of shedding the uterine lining from the previous month in preparation for forming another one. Hopefully, this will be the time when one of your champion swimmers will be making its way to a fertilized egg. Whether or not it was planned, keep your fingers crossed that this might be the month it happens.

WEEK TWO: IN ANTICIPATION OF OVULATION

At this point during week 2, there is still no fetal development. One of her eggs is maturing and getting ready to drop. The lining of her uterus is actually growing thicker in preparation for the new life that will form, which commences with the release of the egg into the fallopian tube around the end of week 2.

Fun fact: Once the egg is released, it can survive for 12 to 24 hours after ovulation, which is when it is most capable of fertilization. Your sperm, on the other hand, can survive in the fertile cervical mucus for up to five days. Those are some durable little swimmers, aren't they? You and your partner can discuss when would be the ideal time to have sex around the ovulation period. This doesn't have to be on the exact day of her ovulation. If you guys can get steamy in the bedroom at least a day or two before the egg is released, it gives the sperm a chance to get in position and begin running the race to the finish line—the egg—once it is released. Only one out of the millions of contestants will be the sweepstakes winner by making it to the fallopian tube and entering the egg. This union is what is referred to as fertilization (Pevzner, 2021).

During her second week, the ovulation process will be marked by a few symptoms. Some will be unmistakable, while others will be harder to discern, but either way, it lets you know that now is the prime time for pregnancy. Here are some common symptoms to look out for:

- **Cervical Changes:** One of the most important changes will be in your partner's cervix as ovulation approaches. Her body has an innate reaction at this time and turns her once thick and sticky cervical mucus to a watery, raw egg-white like substance. Herein is where the atmosphere is created for sperm to survive and, eventually, fertilize an egg.
- **Increased Sex Drive:** The raging hormones of your partner will be evident leading up to ovulation. But don't be alarmed. It's not the

kind of hormonal fluctuation that makes you retreat from sporadic changes in mood. On the contrary, these strong hormonal urges will put your partner in the mood by increasing her sexual desire at the most fertile point of her menstrual cycle. As everything falls into place in the bedroom, the same will be done for the conception of your baby.

- **Mittelschmerz:** Also considered ovulation pain, or middle pain, this is described as a sharp pain on the lower side of the abdomen. The temporary pains only last for a few days and can vary in intensity or may not come at all depending on the person. However, you want to be careful of this as a tell-tale sign since abdomen aches can also be caused by gas or nausea.

This may be an exciting time for both you and your partner, especially if you're actively trying to get pregnant. It's also in your partner's best interest that you encourage them to maintain a balanced diet and get an exercise routine going. When your partner's stress levels are low and energy levels are high, it adds to her estrogen increase and strengthens your connection, making intimacy between the two of you effortless and

VIRGIN DAD | 19

something to be desired. On the contrary, when your partner experiences high levels of stress, whether it's coming from work, financial concerns, or anxiety over the thought of becoming pregnant, this can negatively impact fertility and lower sex drive.

You can counter these stressors by going for walks, taking your partner out to dinner, having a relaxing day at the beach, or planning an outing with friends and family. An atmosphere of serenity needs to be maintained as much as possible when you're aiming to shoot and not miss the target with pregnancy.

With your newfound understanding of the timing of your partner's ovulation, neither of you wants to make the mistake of being too calculated with intimacy. This will ruin the spontaneity of lovemaking and leave your sex life rigid and unsatisfying. The only preparation you need to think about is trying to conceive during the peak of your partner's fertility.

Depending on your partner's cycle, her peak fertility would be at least two days before she ovulates. If your partner's cycle is regular (typically 28 days), she is likely to be most fertile between day 12 and day 14. If she has an irregular cycle, which tends to be longer, then she would ovulate later in the cycle. Remember that this is intimacy, not a weekly exercise routine. So, keep the mood fun, fresh, and light and watch how it all works out in perfect timing.

WEEK THREE: THE PERFECTLY IMPERFECT CONCEPTION

The bedroom activities being practiced by you and your partner may be anything but immaculate, but that doesn't mean that your conception will be anything short of the perfect gift for both of you. Not everyone scores a shot at the three-point line on their first attempt, so having your spouse take a home pregnancy test to be sure is perfectly fine before organizing a trip to the doctor. However, be certain to test at the correct time, as testing too soon will result in a false negative result or what is known as a "faint line," leaving you unclear of your conception status.

Now would be the time to get excited if you haven't already. You're one step closer to being a father. In week three, once fertilization has been completed, the process continues, and the egg now implants itself along the lining of your partner's uterus. This implantation would cause your partner to experience cramping as well as light spotting, or implantation bleeding, which only occurs in one out of five women. So, if your wife happens to experience any spotting, you can reassure her that it's just a part of the process.

If, however, she experiences pain along with the bleeding, take the initiative and contact her doctor immediately as it may signal an ectopic pregnancy. An ectopic pregnancy happens when a fertilized egg implants and grows outside the wall of the uterus, which should be treated as a medical emergency since it can cause the fallopian tube to rupture or damage the surrounding organs. These consequences can lead to fatal internal bleeding and should be dealt with promptly. A few other primary symptoms you may notice during this period include:

- **Bloating:** A release of the hormone progesterone in the early stages of pregnancy causes the muscles to feel relaxed, including those in the digestive tract, which leads to gas and abdominal bloating. This may cause your wife to feel uncomfortable and can even cause constipation. The best way to counter this situation would be to keep her hydrated and fed with lots of high-fiber foods like fruits, vegetables, whole grains, and nuts.
- **Sore Breasts:** Not only will her senses be heightened, but your spouse will also experience an exaggerated soreness around her breasts. Her breasts may feel tender and

sensitive, while some women also experience a darkening of their nipples.

- **Nausea:** Dealing with morning sickness? Another early symptom and unmistakable sign of pregnancy is nausea. But contrary to its name, morning sickness can strike at any time —morning, noon, or night!

Around the end of the third and into the fourth week, the new life inside of your spouse is developing into a blastocyst, in the shape of a tiny ball made up of hundreds of cells. These cells aid in creating the embryo and the placenta that will be the baby's lifeline and source of oxygen and nutrients, as well as a passage to dispose of its toxic waste. As you can tell, quite a lot can happen in just three weeks!

WEEK FOUR: WHEN IN DOUBT, TAKE A TEST

Signs and symptoms may be enough to convince you, but it's always wise to get a pregnancy test done. An at-home pregnancy test relies on the release of the hormone, human chorionic gonadotropin (hCG), which results in the line being positive or negative. Even if your partner has already taken a pregnancy test that turned out to be positive, take it a step further by going to the doctor for a professional opinion. It won't hurt to get an update on the progress that is being made with your tiny embryo. And as we've learned, not every woman's period cycle is the same. Despite seeing all the symptoms mentioned previously in week three, allow a licensed doctor to give you a professional diagnosis of your partner's current pregnancy status as well as an estimated due date (Donaldson-Evans, 2021).

The reason why it's so common to get tested at this time is that week four is when most women experience a missed period, which is arguably the most conspicuous sign of impregnation. This is a crucial time for mommy and baby; both should be given special care and attention. Although most women mistakenly mark the beginning of their pregnancy as the fourth week, the precise count would be her first month. This means there are only eight more to go! Let's take a look at this week's development:

- **PMS-Like Mood Swings:** It's something you might dread having to deal with, but it would be best to prepare for your wife's sporadic mood changes. Be compassionate with her, as she is undergoing major changes both physically and emotionally. And since you aren't the one bearing the responsibility of actually carrying a growing fetus inside of you, it's hard to know exactly what she's feeling. Be patient with her and use every opportunity to lighten the mood.

- **Missed period:** Realizing that your partner has missed her period is the single most obvious sign that the pregnancy is official. If she's keeping track of her cycle, this is your biggest confirmation of a possible pregnancy. Some women encounter other symptoms before a missed period, so it's in your best interest to take all variables into account.

- **Growth of the Embryo:** The embryo has made its way from the fallopian tube and has already implanted itself in your spouse's uterine lining, where it will remain lodged for the next eight months. The blastocyst separates itself at this stage—part of it becomes the embryo, while the other half becomes the placenta. Though the embryo is still quite small—only about 1 millimeter long—an amazing amount of work is being done to set up shop in mommy's stomach until the delivery date.

- **Development of the Amniotic Sac:** Also known as the water bag, the amniotic sac begins to form around the embryo. This is also the time at which the yolk sac forms and acts as a nutrition and gas transfer between mommy and baby before the placenta takes over as the main lifeline after the first trimester. It's vital to be selective about the food your wife is consuming, as she will literally be sharing *EVERYTHING* she eats with your rapidly growing baby (Weiss, 2021).

Stepping up and Quitting Bad Habits

Your spouse's maternal instincts will probably start kicking in by now. She may not even have a visible bump yet, but believe me when I say, the world is already beginning to revolve around this baby.

You should adopt a similar approach as well. During the first trimester, your spouse is experiencing a mix of emotions and symptoms. One such symptom is fatigue, which means you will find her resting more than usual. Hormonal changes, a plethora of overwhelming thoughts, and a rapidly transforming body will begin to take their toll on her. And let's not forget the frequent visits to the bathroom. All of these can leave her drained.

When her tiredness becomes more evident, offer to do things like vacuum or sweep the floor. If your spouse doesn't clean the house, will it become a pigsty? To avoid that, offer to split the chores with her (Durocher, 2020).

☆ A PERSONAL STORY

I can remember how it was for my wife and me when we first found out she was pregnant. Not that we didn't see it coming because we're never stingy when it comes to affection. If I said I took it like a champ, I'd be lying. It went a little something like this:

So, there I was, laying on the couch after a hard day of work, watching TV. She walked in, didn't say anything and handed me a stick. I had no idea what it was.

"So, we're drawing sticks to decide who's doing the dishes now?" I asked unassumingly, hardly looking to consider what was in my hand. After a few seconds of nothing but silence from my wife, I looked her way to see mixed emotions of anxiety, excitement, joy, and anticipation all in one pensive stare. Returning my gaze to the stick that I held, I looked at it, trying to figure out what it was. Then, it suddenly dawned on me.

"Wait... You're...?"

"Pregnant!" She blurted it out in tears, unable to contain her enthusiasm.

"Why are you crying?" I asked, unsure of how I should respond, as this would be our first child together.

"Why aren't you crying?" she replied, expecting me to share in the same rush of emotion.

Not wanting to ruin the moment, I responded with the only thing I knew wouldn't raise any unwanted suspicion, "I'm... just in a state of shock!" I said genuinely. And truly, I was. We'd always discussed how life would be with an addition to our family—a girl for her and a boy for me. But life and careers had kept us so busy that it'd been chopped down to wishful thinking.

As if she'd been reading my mind, she said, "We've been talking about having a baby for so long now … and it's finally happening!" she said, smiling, obviously ecstatic about the new revelation.

My heart was pounding in my chest as I realized that I was about to be a father. I tried to be present with her in this blissful moment that we would remember for our entire lives, but my excitement quickly turned to over-analyzing as I considered the preparation that would need to go into ensuring Susan got the best care possible, for her and the baby.

"How are you so sure, though? When was your last period supposed to start?" I asked casually, trying not to seem like a nervous wreck.

"About three days ago. When I noticed it was late the first day, I didn't pay it much mind. But by day two, I suspected something was different. I even threw up a bit at work last week ... I thought it was the leftover potato salad, but it turned out to be ... something I wasn't expecting" she replied. I could sense the despondence in her voice as she looked away to the empty room behind me, which we decided would be for a baby, eventually.

Not wanting her to feel that I was disappointed by the pregnancy, I said, "Hey ... I want this just as much as you do. Being that this is our first time expecting a baby, I'm just thinking ahead, you know? I'm going to need to work a few extra hours to make sure you're covered for doctor visits. Speaking of which, we're going to need to get you scheduled to see how everything is going in there."

She looked at me and smiled nervously, as if taken aback by my response. "I'm just glad you're taking this well. My girlfriend told me the moment her husband found out she was pregnant, he wanted her to get an abortion. He said he was about to get a promotion and having a baby would ruin his chances. Now, she's heartbroken because she wanted a family." She looked down and started to tear up again. "So ... I guess ... I'm just glad to know you're in this together with me." Her voice broke as a tear streamed from her left eye.

"Susan … " I moved closer to console her. "Even if I got a promotion right now, I would never put that over you … or this family," I reassured her, placing my hand gently on her stomach. "A baby is a blessing. And I know we'll get through this together."

That was how I avoided putting my head on the chopping block when I found out my wife was pregnant. That was our first child, and although we were just starting our life in a less than ideal financial situation, we had faith that things would get better. And they did! But my response was crucial in that moment. If I displayed anything less than being responsible and supportive, the outcome would've been drastically different.

So, to all the future and present fathers reading this, of all the times to be hyper-emotional and in your feelings —now isn't the time for that. Am I saying not to be vulnerable with your partner? Not at all. However, I am advising that you show yourself as strong, understanding, dependable, responsible, and action oriented as your partner will need you to keep a level head while she is dealing with a rollercoaster of emotions. You may also be battling internally with all sorts of emotions of your own, but it's never wise to be led by your emotions, especially when you need to be thinking logically for your family.

QUESTIONS AND ANSWERS: WHAT FATHERS NEED TO KNOW

Question:

1. Is it logical to take more than one pregnancy test?
2. What should I or shouldn't I say to my newly pregnant partner?
3. How does she want me to act?
4. What can I do to be supportive?

Answers:

1. At-home pregnancy tests are about 97% accurate, according to the American Pregnancy Association. But that means nothing if your partner tests too early, which can lead to false-negative results. If the timing of ovulation is right and your partner's test comes back negative, she should wait until a few days later to try again.
2. Just as there are topics you want to avoid when building attraction with someone you

like, there are responses you want to avoid giving after learning of your spouse's pregnancy. You want to steer clear of questions like "Are you sure?"; "But weren't you on the pill?"; "How could this happen?"; "Are you sure it's mine?"; or simply remaining silent. These answers communicate doubt and insecurity, two mindsets your spouse doesn't need.

3. Even if the pregnancy wasn't planned, the best thing to do is to be supportive. Express your concern for your partner and your willingness to help her through this time. After all, both of your actions led to this outcome, so she's expecting you to step up and be responsible as a man.

4. Support can be shown in a variety of ways. Simply showing interest by accommodating her lifestyle change can show support. Monitor her caffeine intake, discontinue the drinking of alcohol, ensure that she isn't receiving any second-hand smoke if you are a smoker, and do your best to give her nutrient-rich foods. Accompany her to doctor's visits, encourage and reassure her, express your love by showing affection, and encourage her to get enough rest. Help around the house with cooking and

cleaning and stay up to date with her and the baby's progress.

You made it through the first month, which basically means you found out she is pregnant and are now buckled into the rollercoaster for the remainder of the ride.

2

LET ME HOLD YOUR HAIR BACK— THE SECOND MONTH

WEEK FIVE: EVOLUTION NOW!

It's week five in the pregnancy and you're about to start witnessing even more remarkable changes in your partner. If you thought the morning sickness and mood swings were something to deal with, you've only just begun experiencing changes. In the words of Nick Bolt, " When you lean over to your pregnant wife to say I love you and she instantly replies with 'chips and dip,' then you know she's pregnant." In other words, brace for impact! The journey into pregnancy is only just beginning for your partner (and you by extension), so being the supportive and proactive man that you are, there are a few things about this time that you should be aware of! Remember that this is a joint effort, and your spouse needs your support in every way possible.

First, if your spouse's pregnancy test has, for whatever reason, returned as negative despite experiencing all or most of the symptoms we have listed thus far, then now would be a great time for another test just to be certain. This is the time when the hCG hormone is strongest, which is the hormone responsible for determining the color of the test result.

At five weeks, your spouse will be feeling a stronger connection, emotionally and physically, with the growing embryo at this time. Although it's not visible to the naked eye and definitely not in the form of a baby bump, don't be deceived. A massive amount of growth is being done under the surface.

Your Baby

You may be surprised to know that at five weeks, or month 2 of your pregnancy, your baby measures no more than 1.5 mm. That's about the size of an orange seed—great things do come in small packages! Nevertheless, the baby is growing at a rapid rate, and the major and minor systems in its body, specifically the circulatory, digestive, and nervous systems, are beginning to form. As a result, the organs that are also used primarily in these bodily systems, namely the brain, heart, lungs, and stomach, are also being developed simultaneously. If you have scheduled an ultrasound to get a visual of your joint creation in progress, you stand the chance of hearing a heartbeat toward the end of the week, although it's most common around the six to seven-week period.

Another essential organ that's under development besides the heart, lungs, and stomach at this time is the brain. The neural tube is the infant stage of the baby's fully matured brain and spinal cord, so it's especially important to accommodate your partner and ensure that you keep her smiling, her mind at ease, and her body rested during this crucial time of evolution (WhattoExpect, 2014).

While your partner is undergoing all these changes internally (meaning inside her stomach), it may come as a shock to know that your shared speck of life has actually taken on the form of a tadpole! Not to say that you should be expecting anything less than a prince or a princess in the next seven months, but the embryo will now actually have a tail. The neural tube I mentioned earlier runs from the top to the bottom of the embryo, giving it the appearance of a tadpole. It's truly marvelous that a fully functioning baby can be produced from something that seems so formless. In the coming weeks, you will bear witness to how this

precursor organism transforms into your eagerly anticipated baby.

Now, despite how elementary and unseemly the baby
may look at this stage, it's not in vain. I mentioned
earlier that the body's primary systems, such as the
nervous, circulatory, and digestive systems, would
begin their formation in the embryo at this time. As
small as it may seem, the embryo will be split into three
layers to form those systems from the inside. They go
as follows:

- **Ectoderm:** This makes up the outer layer of the
  embryo and is responsible for forming the
  nervous system. That includes the baby's spinal
  cord and brain, as well as its skin, hair, and
  nails.
- **Mesoderm:** The mid-layer, also known as the
  mesoderm, is tasked with developing the
  circulatory system, consisting mainly of the
  baby's heart and blood. Also included in this
  germ-layer development are the bones,
  muscles, and kidneys.
- **Endoderm:** The inner layer, also known as the
  endoderm, is the inner-most of all three layers
  and will be transformed into your baby's lungs,
  intestines, and liver. Going further, the
  endoderm forms a tissue called the epithelium,

which tightly binds cells together to form
sheets that form the lining of the gut, which
houses organs like those previously mentioned.

Symptoms to Expect at Week 5

Houston, we have some progress! As we have found out at the start of the chapter, progress is being made in your partner's pregnancy whether you notice it or not. Chances are, many of the changes around the fifth week will be subtle, while other changes will be more overt. Now that you have an idea of what's happening beneath the surface of your partner's seemingly calm exterior, let's look at a few symptoms that even you won't be able to miss at this time:

- **Strong Pregnancy Hormones:** Much of the changes taking place in your partner, such as the soreness in her breasts, increase in breast size due to tissue growth, and the development of the placenta, are all activated by the mass release of hormones such as estrogen, progesterone, and hCG. It's safe to say that her hormones are in overdrive right now, which could be bittersweet if you're on the receiving end of her mercurial moods. This brings me to the next visible change—her rollercoaster of emotions.

- **Emotional Extremes:** The probability of PMS-like mood swings was discussed as something to be expected in week four of pregnancy, but this can spill over into week five depending on the ovulation cycle. Besides an irregular ovulation cycle, the release of the main sex hormone in women, estrogen, can also be the reason for fluctuating emotions. Plus, merely the thought of being an expecting mother can be enough to leave your spouse's mind in a daze. She's contemplating whether or not she is ready for such a huge life change and going from ecstatic with joy to worrisome and regretful. This is bound to affect her moods, which is perfectly normal. Remember to be understanding and patient with your partner, as I'm sure these thoughts and more have traversed your mind as well!

- **Fatigue:** With so many complex processes at play in your partner's body to accommodate the new life being formed, it's a given that she would be experiencing fatigue. If you've ever gone to the gym, you understand how spent your body is after hitting a set of dumbbell curls. If your muscles feel sore and your body taxed after a day in the gym, imagine how it must feel when an entirely new life is being cultivated inside of you. Her fatigue is just an outward manifestation of the physical and emotional changes she is feeling (Pevzner, 2021).

Tips to Make It Through Week 5

As things are beginning to progress rapidly for both the baby and mommy, there are a few tips you might want to consider to make life a bit more manageable for your spouse. Here are a few health and household practices you can implement along with your partner:

- **Do's and Don'ts in the Kitchen:** If there's one thing you probably won't need to remind your partner of it is going to be her distaste for meat like chicken, fish, or beef, especially when raw or undercooked. Sorry, but that means no sushi takeout. Regardless of them being a great source of protein, it's best for her to avoid these types of food early in the pregnancy. Included in her list of off-limit foods are unpasteurized dairy products, undercooked eggs, mercury-dense fish, raw fish, hotdogs and other deli meats, caffeine, and alcohol. Some of the foods mentioned contain nitrates and nitrites, which are said to be the cause of an early delivery.

- **Foods That Cause Bloating:** The best protein substitutes would be yogurt, beans, or soy products like tofu and edamame. Vegetable options for protein like carrots, yams, cantaloupe, mangoes, peaches, and apricots are not only great substitutes, but they're also extremely healthy. You should also be aware that bloating is a major symptom during this period. And while eating healthy foods should be a priority for your spouse and baby, steer clear of vegetables like cabbage, cauliflower, and broccoli as they contribute to bloating and gas.

That just about covers it for week 5 of the pregnancy journey. The information provided here should prepare you for any hiccups along the way. Keep a positive attitude and you, your spouse, and your baby will make it through these crucial periods.

WEEK SIX

Great! You have made it to the six-week mark together despite being a bit inexperienced.

Your Baby

Regardless of its miniscule size, your baby's heart is actually beating nearly twice as fast as yours. Talk about putting in extra work! The parts of the body needed for the five senses are now being developed, including the vocal cords inside the mouth and the arms and legs, although those appear more like the stunted limbs of a T-Rex. That won't last for long, though, as those paddle-shaped arms and legs will stretch in length to full-grown limbs. In addition, the backbone extends into a curve that takes on the appearance of a small tail at the tip of the bone. Most size descriptions compare your baby to a lentil at this stage, but a germinating kidney bean would be a more accurate description of what the baby resembles at six weeks of development.

Symptoms to Expect at Week 6

Now that we have an update on the baby's growth progress, what can we say about mommy's changing features in week six? To be honest, the symptoms are much the same with only a few new ones that may now begin to surface. Your partner will have already started experiencing the more common side effects like fatigue, mood swings, nausea, sore breasts, and bloating as we've mentioned in the previous weeks. However, some are worth reiterating, as there may be solutions you can suggest to your partner, provided you don't offer it during a volatile mood swing!

- **Morning Sickness:** The truth about morning sickness is that, while doctors aren't certain of what causes the discomfort, it makes sense that hormones are to blame. While it was also mentioned as a symptom in week three, it's important to note that it could last up to three months (the entire first trimester) of her pregnancy. Since there is a lack of scientific data identifying the actual cause of morning sickness, there isn't much that can be done to prevent it (Gates, 2022). However, there are methods to soothe an upset stomach, such as trying a protein-rich snack like granola and yogurt or opting for a smoothie or soup instead of solids. So, if your partner is feeling queasy and you're the one in the kitchen, offer her these options. Or if you decide to cook solid food, be sure to use ginger in whatever you're doing, whether that be tea, soup, biscuits, or a smoothie. The next time you visit her practitioner, you might want to suggest asking for a vitamin B6 supplement or switching her prenatal vitamin from one high in iron to one higher in vitamin B6.

- **Metallic Taste:** Pregnancy hormones, especially estrogen, are responsible for more side effects than just mood swings in your partner. You're aware now that during the first trimester, there is a surge in estrogen to accommodate the growth of the embryo and the establishment of the placenta, which will essentially be the baby's lifeline. But the sudden spike in her hormones could also cause a strange, metallic taste to linger in her mouth. This symptom is known as *dysgeusia*, a taste disorder that some expecting women must deal with during the first trimester of pregnancy. This is also accompanied by unusual cravings that may send you on a wild goose chase looking for uncommon taste combinations. So, prepare to be hurled out of bed at 1:00 AM with food requests.

- **Frequent Urination:** During the earlier stages of the pregnancy, you may begin to believe that your partner and the bathroom have a secret love affair because she'll be spending much more time in there than normal. Of course, this is no fault of her own. While her hormones may be partly to blame for her frequent tinkle trips to the toilet, the urge to urinate more often is due to the increase of blood flowing through her body, which in turn sends her kidneys into overdrive processing all the extra fluid. Once again, she is undergoing a massive transition with the added pressure of another person being formed inside her body, so it's working to accommodate her and the growing baby. This is especially true if you've been feeding her lots of smoothies and other liquids (Donaldosn-Evans, 2021b). Despite the urge to pee often, keep encouraging her to drink enough water since she needs to be drinking enough to keep herself and the baby hydrated. As you may know, water oxygenates the blood and ultimately produces a higher blood volume. This is essential for providing the baby with the oxygen and nutrients he/she needs to grow strong and healthy. Another significant purpose of water intake during pregnancy would be to avoid constipation and hemorrhoids. Furthermore, as the baby increases in size, your partner will undoubtedly have additional weight to carry around later in the pregnancy, which may lead to swollen feet and ankles. To avoid these issues, the American College of Obstetricians and Gynecologists (ACOG) recommends that pregnant women drink an average of ten 8-ounce cups of water or any other liquid per day, although this should not include caffeinated or alcoholic beverages. An easy way of knowing if your spouse is well-hydrated is through the color of her urine. If it's pale yellow or colorless, then you know she's in the clear. If it's dark yellow, she needs to sip some more liquid.

She may also be experiencing similar symptoms from previous weeks, such as morning sickness, fatigue, and mood swings. Additional symptoms may also include strange dream encounters, which come as a result of her subconscious trying to keep up with the rapid life changes she is facing. The dreams may also be the result of your partner's anxieties regarding motherhood, the birth itself, or the transition of her body during this period.

WEEK SEVEN

Upon exiting the sixth week of pregnancy alongside your spouse, if you haven't already planned a prenatal doctor's visit for your partner, then now would be the perfect time to do so. Yes, even if you two have gotten a positive pregnancy test result that has you feeling confident everything is going according to plan (or at least falling into place despite being unplanned). Getting a doctor's confirmation won't hurt at all, and it'll probably answer a few of the questions you've been dying to ask.

This visit will be long and quite extensive, so prepare to be there for the long haul. Upon arrival, your spouse will undergo a thorough physical consisting of a Pap smear, pelvic exam, and blood test to identify her blood type, as well as to determine whether she is iron deficient. The doctor will also be checking to see if your growing child is currently at risk of any chromosomal abnormalities.

In addition, to ensure the welfare of your spouse and the baby, a test will be conducted for sexually transmitted infections and other genetically inherited ethnic-specific diseases. A sample of her pee will also need to be taken to determine her glucose levels, protein, red and white blood cells, and bacteria. As stated, this being your first visit together, your spouse (and you) can expect this to be an extensive examination loaded with questions surrounding health histories and potential health risks. It may also interest you to organize a questionnaire of your own, especially if the two of you are sharing the same living space. Don't hesitate to ask about the continuation of your sex life, like whether having sex will hurt the baby or how often you can have sex. And, of course, whatever you do or don't ask for will be available in this book as a guide.

So, if you get cold feet and forget to inquire about your concerns, you're still covered!

Your Baby

Now that we've got that out of the way, let's look at what you and your partner can be expecting in week 7 of the pregnancy experience:

- **Baby Got Back:** A week has passed, and you are now at 7 weeks. You might be saying to yourself, "Doesn't sound like much. How much can happen in one week?" And in response to that, I would say you'd be absolutely amazed to find out! In terms of size, the baby is now about the size of a blueberry. That might not sound too extravagant, I know, but consider that your little peanut is now 10,000 times bigger than it was a month ago. If that isn't enough to WOW you, remember that only a week ago, your little peanut was smaller than a peanut—more like the size of a lentil. So there definitely has been remarkable progress taking place (Donaldson-Evans, 2021c). All this additional size isn't just for show. Your baby genius is going to have the brains to match mommy and daddy's good looks too; much of the growth is being condensed in the head area where new cells are being produced rapidly at an average rate of 250,000 cells per minute. At this point, the neural tube that ran from the bottom to the top of the embryo has now closed at both ends, forming the spinal column with the brain at the top. The reason why such a large number of cells are being directed to the brain is that it is currently made up of three areas—the forebrain, midbrain, and hindbrain.

- **The Baby Is Taking Shape:** Good things come to those who wait. And while two months seems like nothing, you're finally going to start seeing the first glimpses of the semblance of an actual baby and not just an unrecognizable embryo. In addition to brain development, the arms and legs are now beginning to sprout and stretch into a more defined shape of limbs although they still vaguely look like paddles. And that's not all that's gaining definition. The mouth, ears, and eyes are also beginning to have more pronounced features. In the coming weeks, your little prince or princess will be able to see and hear the activities within their environment (Gates, 2022a).
- **Kidneys Intact:** Along with the forming of the mouth and tongue is the esophagus, which is used to transport the food received from the

nutrition source (Mommy) to the digestive system. This newly formed digestive system also includes the recently formed stomach and kidneys. With the baby's stomach and kidneys now in place, the process of waste disposal can now begin. This means that the baby will soon be producing urine. Realistically, your child won't need their digestive system until after birth. As long as they're in the womb, the placenta will provide them with all the nutrients needed for survival and growth through the bloodstream of their walking incubator—Mommy.

Symptoms to Expect at Week 7

Just as it was for the previous weeks, the second month of your partner's pregnancy will bring with it its own set of issues. Certain symptoms last throughout the entire first trimester. However, there are a few symptoms reserved for this time that may take you by surprise.

- **Breast Changes:** We went over the tenderness and sensitivity of your wife's breasts previously, but seeing them swollen in size could have you wanting to have a baby again sooner rather than later! It's been determined that progesterone and estrogen are to blame for the itchy, tingly feeling she's been getting. But the increase in breast size may be due to fat build-up and increased blood flow to the same area. Her nipples are likely to be protruding more than ever before, and there will be changes to the areola as well. The dark shade around the nipple, will get even darker with time. All of this occurs in preparation for breastfeeding your newborn when they are delivered in the next seven months.

- **Sudden Food Aversions:** Imagine going from being unable to eat a sandwich without mayonnaise to becoming unsettled in the guts by even being close enough to smell it? That's exactly what your partner is going through right now. It's not a simple love/hate relationship with food; these sudden changes are called food aversions, and they are common in pregnant women. Since most of the cooking will be delegated to you, Top Chef, it may get confusing for you to know which foods to cook for her, as she will likely be turned off by her once-favorite food in favor of something that is completely foreign to her diet. Or she may be repulsed by the food she was once fond of in exchange for … nothing. You may be surprised to find that your spouse's meals have become bland and boring, all to avoid nausea. You will also be tasked with finding substitute foods for your partner to replace the specific foods she finds repulsive. For example, if she used to love fried turkey bacon for breakfast and now, she can't come within five feet of a slice of raw meat, she may have to substitute it for black beans or chickpeas, which are excellent sources of protein. However, her aversions may be a blessing in disguise if she is resistant to foods she should already be avoiding, such as sushi, spicy food, coffee, and raw meat.

- **Heartburn:** In addition to other common symptoms like excessive saliva, heartburn (also known as indigestion or acid reflux) is also an unavoidable and uncomfortable reality every expecting mom will have to face. Since it can't be eradicated, the next best thing to do is to reduce its effect. At your own risk, you can advise your partner to avoid drinks that upset her stomach (like sodas and coffee), eat smaller meal portions, use less acidic foods when cooking, drink liquids in between meals, and ensure that she eats at least two or three hours before going to bed.

- **Keen Sense of Smell**: This symptom is closely linked to food aversions since your partner will be more likely to smell the food develops a distaste for before she recognizes how much it makes her want to gag. Her abhorrence of certain smells will again be the cause of an influx of the estrogen and progesterone hormones that are flooding her body at this time to assist in the rapid growth of the embryo as well as the preparation of her body for post-labor nurturing. Her heightened sense of smell may also be directed toward you, your pets, or other household fragrances. And don't be alarmed in thinking that the intimacy between you two will be ruined. This reaction to her hormone spike is only for a set amount of time, so you'll be back to the bedroom activities before you know it!

Savoring the Cravings

When it comes to her untamed cravings during pregnancy, you stand a better chance of convincing a 6-year-old that eating Skittles will keep their growth stunted for life than reasoning with your spouse that eating a bucket of spicy chicken wings is a bad idea! During this time, she wants what she wants, and there's no stopping her until she gets it. A woman's pregnancy cravings can drive her to indulge in foods from salt-and-vinegar-soaked pickles, chocolate, fruits, and lemons to red meat, fresh fish, intensely spicy dishes, soda, ice, and dairy products. You can also expect strange food combinations or, in extreme cases, non-edible items such as chalk, toothpaste, and baby powder. It goes without saying that you would want to dissuade her from ingesting the latter.

As the other responsible adult in the pregnancy, you want to try your best to encourage her indulgence of healthy cravings. That depends, of course, on your definition of healthy. If you're lucky enough that her cravings are for fruits and vegetables, then let her rip! These foods are undoubtedly beneficial for her and the baby, and the high fiber content will fight against constipation.

But if her cravings go to the extreme opposite, like guzzling packets of sour-cream potato chips or bags of sugar-frosted cereal flakes, then it's time to get creative and suggest some similar, but healthier, alternatives. Instead of sugary frosted flakes, swap out for an oat bran cereal topped with strawberry slices and drizzled with agave honey, molasses, or coconut nectar. Instead of traditional potato chips that are probably high in sodium, opt for plantain chips and soy crisps or prepare your own homemade potato chips with a fraction of the salt.

Instead of letting her pig out on a whole cake, find a recipe for healthy oatmeal cookies and add in a few chocolate chips to satisfy her craving or sprinkle dried fruits in her yogurt as opposed to a full-cream vanilla milkshake. After all, chocolate naturally carries a chemical called tryptophan that produces the feel-good chemical in the brain called serotonin, and a happy mommy is a happy baby during pregnancy. But temper that with good judgment, as chocolate is also high in calories when consumed in large quantities.

Whether you look up recipes online or just get creative with your own inventions in the kitchen, you're going to need to get inventive with your food alternatives if her cravings are through the roof!

WEEK EIGHT

We're now at week eight, which means you're well into the second month of your partner's pregnancy. Only 7 more months to go!

Your Baby

As promised, your little one seems to be having a growth spurt every week now. They've graduated from a blueberry in size to a raspberry and are continuing to broaden their territory at a rate of millimeters a day.

More definition is coming to the arms, legs, and back, as well as the detailing of their lips, nose, and eyelids. Not to say that you weren't before, but you can now rejoice over the fact that your baby is taking on the visage of a real-life baby and has morphed a bit from the reptilian-like creature from the Alien vs. Predator movie. Can I get an Amen?!

Although your baby's fingers and toes are still months away from reaching their final stage of maturity, the webbed features have already set the blueprint for a fully functional set of hand and foot extensions. The good news is that the tail end of the neural tube is almost gone. Get excited! With the forming of the hands, feet, fingers, and toes, the baby will confirm their growth with spontaneous movements, even though you or your partner won't be able to feel those movements just yet. With the stretching of the limbs comes a need for more space. This tenant will be demanding more room to accommodate their growth spurt, and Mommy may begin to feel deeper digs as the amniotic fluid increases in the womb, allowing your child to expand their limbs to full capacity (Gates, 2022c).

Fruit: Nature's Favorite Sweet

It would be a dream come true if your partner had a perpetual craving for fruit throughout the pregnancy. Not only are fruits an essential vitamin and nutrient-rich food source, but they're also a natural source of sugar. One of the most important functions of fruit is their high fiber content, which helps to prevent constipation and keeps Mommy's bowels moving regularly.

Another fun fact about fruit is that certain fruits can be used to replace certain vegetables. For example, dried apricots are one of the richest fiber-containing fruits around. If ever your spouse begins to gag at the scent of sweet potatoes or avocados, apricots will make the perfect substitute. The same can be said for spinach as a source of calcium. If she can't stomach it either raw or cooked, then raisins or apricots will again be a decent replacement. Similarly, if the acidity of oranges is causing her indigestion, switching it with yellow or red bell peppers is a great way to ensure she doesn't skip her dose of vitamin C (Donaldson-Evan, 2021).

But even if you both know fruit is one of the best food options, especially for your spouse and the baby, try not to force it into her diet overtly. Keep the mood light and fun by trying different fruit and vegetable dishes that actually taste good to your partner, and she'll love every moment of it.

Symptoms to Expect at Week 8

▷ **You're on Kitty Litter Duty!**

What could possibly be harmful about a cute, cuddly, furry ball of feline … besides their brandishing claws? Ever hear the saying, "Looks can be deceiving?" Well, that fits the cat profile very well. It's not to say that our furry feline friends have malicious intentions, but it's a parasitic infection called toxoplasmosis, found in a cat's fecal matter, that's the biggest threat to your partner and your unborn baby during pregnancy. It's for this reason that, as a preventative measure, if you keep a cat as a pet, you should be the one to clean out the kitty litter from now on.

So, what exactly is toxoplasmosis? According to the Center for Disease Control (CDC), cats become infected by eating infected birds, rodents, reptiles, and other small animals. They then spread the toxoplasmosis through their droppings, which can then be passed on to cat owners when changing their cat litter, to children in a sandbox, or in a garden bed when gardening without gloves. Many people have contracted toxoplasmosis and have not even noticed, thereby becoming immune to its effects. But even if you and your spouse have been considered immune, you still need to protect your unborn baby. And the best way to go about that is to prevent Mom from getting anywhere close to the kitty litter (CDC, 2020).

Eating raw, infected animals isn't the only way a cat can become infected with toxoplasmosis. It can also be transferred through drinking unpasteurized milk, and contaminated water, or eating undercooked meat. And your feline's waste pile isn't the only way it can be transferred either. Toxoplasmosis can also be transferred if you're the one eating raw or uncooked meat or by eating unwashed fruits and vegetables.

However, in keeping with the topic of felines, the good news is that indoor cats are the least likely to carry toxoplasmosis, so giving your beloved furball the boot isn't necessary. Plus, chances are that if you or your partner have been around cats for an extended period of time, you may be immune to it. But it's better to be safe than sorry, so here are a few tips to reduce the spread of toxoplasmosis and exposure to your baby:

- Keep your pregnant spouse away from the cat litter. Adopt its responsibility as your own, at least until well after the pregnancy. Make it mandatory to wear gloves when disposing of cat poop and wash your hands with antibacterial soap immediately after.

- Change the cat litter daily as the Toxoplasma parasite takes 1 to 5 days to become infectious after being defecated by your cat.
- Avoid feeding your cat raw or uncooked meat. Choose approved dry or canned food instead.
- Avoid adopting wild or stray cats. If you already own a cat, keep it indoors.
- If you own a garden or a sandbox, keep a pair of gloves on when touching either one. Also, be sure to wash any freshly picked fruits and vegetables before consuming them, as well as wash your hands thoroughly after gardening.
- This is probably a given, but avoid feeding your partner raw or uncooked meat (Wahlberg, 2021).

Sure, your cat is a member of the family (if you own one), but the safety of your unborn child is much more important. A few months of cat litter changing won't do you any harm, and I'm sure you and your cat will grow a stronger bond during this time!

▷ **Headaches**

Headaches are a common pregnancy symptom during the first trimester. Identifying the triggers of those headaches is a great way of preventing headaches from occurring often. While rest is an important factor during pregnancy, make sure that your partner does not become inactive and that she gets enough exercise, food, and water. The only doctor-approved pain reliever to take during pregnancy is acetaminophen. You want to avoid the use of pain relievers such as aspirin and ibuprofen since you are unsure of the side effects they will have on the baby. The good news is that there are alternatives and natural headache remedies that you may want to explore with your spouse such as relaxation and breathing techniques, light exercises, taking a shower, or comforting her with a massage. That last one might lead to more than you expected, but it's all in the interest of the two loves in your life, right?

▷ Bodyweight and Self-Image

Try your best not to be one of those guys who gets immediately disinterested the moment their partner begins to pack on a few pounds. After all, she is carrying the manifestation of your seed inside her womb, so these few pounds should be given a huge pass. This too shall pass. In any case, the amount of weight your partner stands to gain in pregnancy depends on her pre-pregnancy body-mass index. This is also why regular ultrasounds, even during the early stages of pregnancy, are vitally important, as you want to know if you'll be expecting twins. This will have an impact on your spouse's overall body mass. Nevertheless, at eight weeks, a belly bump is still not visible, but those cravings are real! Her body is undergoing a major transformation that, if you both decide not to reveal it to family and friends, can be successfully hidden under loose-fitting clothes.

▷ **Keep Her Feeling Sexy**

If she begins to grow hyper-conscious about her weight, you want to maintain the spark by making your partner feel loved, wanted, and sexy, despite the changes her body is going through. This has nothing to do with your spouse feeling insecure. She can be the least needy, most confident woman out there, but it shows a great amount of support on your part to remind her through your words and actions that she's still got it going on! And if she does have some insecurities about her weight, then keeping her spirits up by expressing your affection and attraction for her during this time would be a great way of keeping her centered and appreciated.

Just in case you're wondering, here are a few simple things you can do to accomplish that. Take it from me, as you both enter the unfamiliar territory of pregnancy, the uncertainty and anxiety during this period will only strengthen the bond you two share. Here are a few things to keep in mind when aiming to keep your love life sparking!

- **Speak Life to Your Partner:** The saying goes, "Actions speak louder than words," but that doesn't disqualify words from having value. Sometimes, your individual lives and careers can be so demanding that you forget to show affection, even if only through words. If your schedules were busy before finding out about the pregnancy, then it's about to get even more hectic! Reassuring each other with these three magical words, "I Love You," can go a long way in a relationship.

- **Love in the Tub:** Intimacy doesn't always have to begin in the bedroom. Set aside some free time for you and your partner to bond together in a tub of warm water (but not too warm to avoid pregnancy complications). Sure, you can't pop open a bottle of champagne to accentuate the occasion, but you can take turns scrubbing those hard-to-reach places and share a relaxed conversation about your excitement as first or second-time parents. This is also an excellent way of bonding as a family before the baby is even delivered. Inviting children into an atmosphere of peace and love starts from the early stages of pregnancy, and occasions such as these are the best way to start.

- **Dinner for Two (or Three):** Now is the time in which you want to keep things fresh. Make dinner reservations for you and your spouse at your favorite restaurant as a way of igniting the romantic passion the two of you have always shared. I'm sure your baby genius won't mind tagging along for the outing!

- **Massages:** If you're on a budget and saving for doctor's visits, baby clothes, and diapers, then feel free to put your own hands to good use. You may achieve much more than expected with your tender-loving touch, but I'm sure your spouse won't resist an offer to rub her feet, massage her lower back, or gently rub her belly with body oil. If ever her feet become swollen later in the second or third trimester, massaging her ankles will release the tension concentrated in that area from the additional bodyweight by moving out the fluids that have settled.

- **Genuinely Compliment Her:** Your words have the power to either put a smile on someone's face or cause them to sink into a pit of despair.

Realizing the power you wield, use it to boost your partner's self-confidence. Regardless of whether you always see your spouse as the most beautiful apple of your eye, telling her, she's beautiful on occasion could be exactly what she needs to push through on the days when she feels the opposite (Family Education Staff, 2019). We know you're doing the bulk of everything right now, and your selfless actions speak the love language loud enough as it is. But don't forget to back that up with compliments, reassuring her that you're there for her and that you love her no matter what.

▷ Morning Sickness

One of the most insufferable symptoms a woman can experience is morning sickness. Imagine being unable to control your gag reflexes first thing in the morning and throughout the day, where the nausea is constant and you're at the mercy of raging hormones. We, as men, can do nothing to trade places with our spouses and take some of the pain away, nor can we prevent morning sickness altogether. What we can do is try our best to alleviate the effects of morning sickness. We may not be able to put an end to her suffering, but we can do things that help make her experience a little less horrible.

- **Appreciate What She Is Enduring:** The dynamic of how a man and woman are interdependent on each other to create another human being through pregnancy is a wonder that will forever be a fascinating part of creation. It's true that the entire implantation would not be possible without a man's semen, but planting that seed is the easy part. The bulk of the load from thereon is now left to your partner, who's entire being is then centered on nurturing and carrying a life to full term. Understand the enormous responsibility she has in being a walking incubator for nine months. Let her know that you appreciate her bravery in going through with the pregnancy. And while you may not be able to directly share in the ordeal, you admire her strength. Remind her that she is amazing and follow up your words with action by being there for her emotionally whenever she needs a crutch to lean on.

- **Listen and Be Empathetic:** I know it seems impossible in a realistic sense but putting yourself in your partner's shoes is a great way of showing your desire to ease her discomfort. In the same way that wads of money can't buy or replace genuine love, feeding your partner comfort food can't replace giving her your undivided attention. Listen to her grumbling about the way she feels. After all, who else can she vent to besides you?

- **Clean the House:** A relationship is a partnership designed to be a crutch for the weaker person in their time of vulnerability. And if there's any time you will find a woman at her most vulnerable state, it is during pregnancy. More than likely, your spouse is the one who usually does the home cleaning and decorating. But while she can barely get out of bed due to nausea, it's up to you to man the fort. Sure, keeping the house clean will by no means eradicate her morning sickness, but it will give her a chance to rest and relax. As often as you can, wash the dishes, do the laundry, fold the clothes, and ensure the floor is clean during this brief period (Murphy, 2016).
- **Remove All Possible Aversions:** As you are aware by now, the increase of hormones like estrogen and progesterone is the main culprit

for not only morning sickness but also a heightened sense of smell in your spouse. Her heightened sensitivity to scents in the atmosphere also causes her to develop aversions to once-normal foods and household items. Again, this is not a symptom she can fix. For example, the smell of your cologne may have been an attractive scent to your spouse before the pregnancy, but now, she sniffs at its scent. Or perhaps the two of you used to enjoy blended oatmeal and banana smoothies, but now the slightest smell of banana sends her skidding to the toilet bowl. Learning what her aversions are and removing them from the immediate environment is a great way of keeping her from being triggered.

- **Run the Errands:** No matter how much your spouse wants to stop resting so she can take care of bills or bank payments, insist that she stay at home. Why risk her vomiting in the car or at the grocery store? The best thing would be to run the errands yourself. Pick up the groceries, pay her bills, and ensure that she has no worries. Show that you are a responsible adult and that you can do it (Paolelli, 2019)!

▷ **Mood Swings**

At some point in your partner's pregnancy, usually within the first trimester, you're going to have to deal with mood swings. Remaining ignorant about the reason behind those mood swings guarantees that your response will be negative. As we've pointed out already, everything about your spouse is changing right now, and she is under immense amounts of pressure.

The reason for her mood swings is the same reason for her sensitivity to smell and morning sickness—hormones. Her attitude won't remain this way forever, so understanding what's happening, knowing that you're not to blame, and being patient with her through the process will make her transformation much smoother.

This is intended to be a beautiful time for both of you as you welcome a new being into the world that shares a piece of each of you. So, don't let the periodical roller-coaster of emotions put a damper on such a memorable time in both of your lives. Here are a few ways to deal with those emotional twists and turns in the most effective way:

- **Be Patient:** Patience is key in every adverse situation but especially with your pregnant wife's mood swings. Arguing will only make matters worse with no solution. Use this time as a chance to increase your tolerance and level of patience. Knowledge is power, so understanding that her raging hormones are part of the pregnancy process will cause you to respond logically instead of reacting to her emotions.

- **Encourage Healthy Eating**: Refrain from eating junk food or drinking sodas or alcohol in front of her, especially if it's something she loves. Unhealthy food could have a negative effect on her hormones, resulting in even worse mood swings. Instead, accompany her on her healthy eating journey. This is also a way of showing your support for her and the baby's health. On the flip side, low blood sugar is known to cause mood swings, so if you find her being triggered, offer her the pastry she loves or take her for ice cream. But try not to let her overindulge (Lewsley, 2021).

- **It's Not Supposed to Make Sense**: Men like to get to the bottom of everything—we like to know the reason behind a thing. But during your wife's pregnancy, lay your investigative desires to rest because rationale will be useless. Avoid the need to be right or wrong and learn to let things slide for the sake of your spouse during the pregnancy.

- **Express Your Love for Her:** Now, more than ever, your partner needs your moral and physical support. Do your best to make her feel special by maintaining a peaceful, positive, and joyful environment. Offer to do things that will make her day, like cooking her favorite meal or giving her a soothing massage. Don't be reluctant to pamper her because it's needed most in this season. Part of her mood swings may involve a sudden change in likes and dislikes. Try to keep track of those shifts and make the necessary adjustments to keep her happy and at ease.

- **It's Not Personal, Just Pregnancy:** If she's flying off the handle for no apparent reason, even when you've been trying your best to accommodate her, don't be too hard on yourself. Responding to hyper-emotional outbursts with emotions is a recipe for disaster and won't leave you feeling any better about yourself. Remember that her emotions are the result of her hormones, so taking her words and actions personally is pointless. That isn't to say that you are emotionless, just less emotionally invested regarding her attitude at this time.

- **Be Sympathetic:** The moment you understand that she's not just being vindictive or trying to get under your skin out of sheer boredom (especially if this has never been her personality), then it makes sympathizing with her much easier. Keep in mind that she is carrying the child you both share, so try to minimize any potential arguments and let peace reign in the atmosphere for the sake of your son or daughter. Trust me, if you can maintain a level of patience with your partner during the pregnancy, you will have reached guru status!
- **Hang in There:** This may be your first pregnancy experience with your spouse, and you are probably second-guessing your decision to follow through with the pregnancy because of how difficult things are right now. But nothing in life is all peaches and cream. And even if it tastes and feels that way at the beginning, a test is bound to come sooner or later. Enduring pregnancy with your spouse may be the greatest test of your character you have ever had to face in life, but you would be surprised at how you come out of it a better man with more patience, self-control, and

genuine love for your family. So, hang in there, it's only going to get better.

☆ A PERSONAL STORY

I've had my fair share of my wife's mood swings, and to say they left me bewildered, would be a gross under-statement. I made a career out of walking on eggshells. That's how good I got at doing it—all to avoid an argument. I wasn't wise to what was happening in the moment, but it didn't take that long for me to catch on. If my memory serves me correctly, it started like any other day.

One day, my wife came home crying. When I asked her why, she said, "Someday I am going to have a dog, and it is going to die." We hadn't had a dog the entire five years we had been together.

By now, we were two months into the pregnancy, and I was doing all I could to stay on top of things. My superior agreed to give me a few weeks off despite recently being promoted to supervisor, and I wanted her to get as much rest as possible. But where was this talk of dogs coming from? And why was she suddenly in her feelings about a dog? To be honest, I was blindsided.

"But babe … What's important is that we enjoy the time we DO have to spend with the dog. That's what really matters," I said, trying to be sentimental. "If you want a dog, we can get one. That's a great idea! We can get a puppy that'll grow up with the baby!" I was getting excited at the possibility of getting a new dog, and I knew our baby would love it too.

"No! We can't get a dog because it's going to die, and then I'm going to be sad, and the baby will get used to it and have to be sad too … I just don't want to deal with losing another animal!" She cried, drenching her shirt in tears. Then she looked at me with a sorrowful look in her eyes and said, "I'm not going to lose you too, am I? I don't want to lose you too, honey, not now! You're planning to leave me, aren't you? Just like our last dog, right?! You're just going to leave me … to raise our baby alone … in the middle of my pregnancy!" She screamed hysterically, panting heavily while trying to catch her breath through slurred speech.

In shock at how quickly things had escalated, I chose my next words very carefully. As a matter of fact, I was lost for words for the next minute. But I didn't want her to think I was giving her the silent treatment, so I thought fast and hard about my next response. One thing I knew for sure was that matching her emotional tone was a no-no.

"Babe, you know I would never do that. The thought has never even crossed my mind." I replied calmly, thinking to myself why I was suddenly being compared to a dog. I dismissed the thought. "I love being with you throughout this pregnancy. Besides, I'm just not the type of guy to up and leave when times get hard. We've planned what our life would be as a family for years now. We had our fun, and now it's finally happening! Why would I want to miss out on that?" I asked in a probing yet gentle way. My intention was to shift the negative emotional charge to a more peaceful, positive tone.

"Oh, I know, honey," she responded, her face lit up with excitement. At this point, I wasn't sure if I was dealing with my wife or Dr. Jekyll and Mr. Hyde. Nevertheless, it wasn't that serious. She continued, "It's just that I'm throwing up all the time, I'm feeling lazy, and I can feel I'm starting to put on weight. Some men leave when their wives get chunky in pregnancy ... and I don't want that to be us," she explained.

"It won't!" I quickly reassured her, "... be us." I added. "I'm not other guys. And trust me ... I'll love every curve of you regardless of a little baby fat. That's more cushion for me, baby." I said smoothly, caressing her hips and thighs.

She flashed a seductive look at me as if to say, "Come and get it, tiger!" And that night, everybody went to bed satisfied. I'm just glad I listened during the doctor's visit when he said I should be expecting dramatic mood swings. I suppose all's well that ends well. Until the next episode of my wife's emotional rollercoaster!

QUESTIONS AND ANSWERS: WHAT FATHERS NEED TO KNOW

Questions:

1. Does she still like me?
2. Will she feel like having sex again?
3. When should I start preparing financially?
4. How do I know if I will be able to provide financially as well as I should?

Answers:

1. Not only does your partner still like you, but at this point, she's terrified of losing you. The two of you may not be on the same page with everything, and that may be because you're both experiencing the pregnancy from different perspectives. Rest assured, though, her intimacy toward you is growing even stronger now. But be warned, whether it's her first or second pregnancy, her fear of abandonment may cause her to be more clingy

than usual. She just wants to know that she's not in this alone.

2. Despite her raging hormones, sex may slow down due to your partner's feelings of exhaustion and nausea, especially during the first trimester. The rush of hormones can increase her arousal, but as we've learned, things can suddenly go left if she feels overwhelmed, drained, and moody.

3. The moment it's been confirmed that you and your spouse will be expecting a child, it's time to start saving. You're not just preparing for the first few months or two years with diapers, wipes, and meals—you need to start thinking of a financial plan that will cover college tuition! The quicker you can work out financial plans, the more relaxed you will be and the more fun you can have with your newborn.

4. Providing is one thing, but putting the money you earn to good use is something else. Before the baby arrives, sit down with your partner and create a financial plan. Start to budget your money and spend wisely. Pay off any credit card debt, get your credit score up, buy life insurance, and add your baby onto your insurance so that they're also covered. When a baby comes into the picture, it's less about just

working for money and more about how your money can work for you.

The second month can be a difficult time because your partner is obviously going through changes, though you don't necessarily see a physical change yet, so it can be a confusing time.

3

LOVELY BABY BUMPS —THE THIRD MONTH

WEEK NINE

Your Baby

You're now at nine weeks into the pregnancy, which is about the 3rd month mark, and your baby hasn't taken a day off from growing despite your spouse's fatigue. Since the last raspberry measurement, the baby is now roughly an inch long, which is about the size of a green olive. Let's check out the positive progress your little one is making:

- **Becoming a Fetus:** In just one week's time, your little Titan will be graduating from an embryo to a fetus. His features are becoming even more pronounced, such as the visibility of his ears, toes, arms, elbows, knees, and eyelids. That's another step in the right direction to looking more like humanoid offspring! In addition, the organs beneath the surface, like his heart, brain, kidneys, liver, and lungs, are all continuing to develop nicely. One essential organ that's developing even further is your baby's heart. All four chambers of their heart have already formed and have grown large enough and strong enough to be heard clearly.

- **Developing Teeth:** Remember how we mentioned earlier in week six that your baby's esophagus and mouth were being formed and sculpted? Well, there are even more features added now! Inside the mouth of your fetus, tooth buds are beginning to form that will harden not long from now to form along their jaw. This is all in preparation for post-delivery, when your baby receives their first tooth between 4 and 7 months of age.

- **Placenta Is in Full Effect:** As promised, at the end of the first trimester, the yolk sac has handed its duties over to the placenta, which has now been attached to the uterus and will be functioning as the nutrition and gas transfer to the baby through the umbilical cord. Part of the job of the placenta also includes producing the hormones needed for the baby to develop further. Another sweet victory as you head into the coming months with your baby (Marple, 2022).

Symptoms to Expect at Week 9

- **The Fatigue is Real:** Pregnancy is not for the weak of heart. But because of the great love of a mother for her child, your spouse has no problem going through with it, right? As the baby grows inside of her, it's expected that they will also increase in size, which she is probably not too ecstatic about. The weight is more than likely becoming visible and her clothes are becoming tight. Not to mention that she is peeing more than a sailor at a beach bar. Although it's not seen with the naked eye (at least not for another 6 months), making a baby is hard work, and her extreme fatigue is just one major sign of it. Her body has been working twice as hard in recent weeks for the placenta to begin fully functioning. And because her body is working overtime for her and the baby, it has caused her metabolism and hormone levels to increase dramatically, which in turn lowers blood sugar, resulting in fatigue.

At this point, you want to ensure that she is being fed a balanced diet to normalize her blood sugar and blood pressure levels. An increased amount of blood, nutrients, oxygen, and water is required for the development of the baby. And as you might imagine, the more the baby grows, the more of these vital ingredients are required. So, if you find that your partner is dragging her feet out of bed, you can be hopeful that it won't last for very long. The good news is that the extreme fatigue and morning sickness will begin to return to some level of normalcy over the next few weeks when the placenta is in its final stages of completion. However, this reprieve is short-lived, as the fatigue returns in the third trimester when the much larger fetus will demand more physical vitality in preparation for delivery (Donaldson-Evans, 2021d).

- **Remedy for Aching Breasts:** Let's keep it real —you're the only one in the relationship who is enjoying the hearty shape of your partner's breasts at this time. You probably haven't seen them this plump before. But that doesn't take away from the fact that she may be feeling aches or sharp, stabbing pains in that area. As we've learned in the previous chapter, this is occurring because of the fat build-up and the blood flow stored around her breasts in preparation for feeding once the baby is born. To alleviate the pain she is feeling right now, use an ice pack wrapped in a towel and place it on the sore area to lessen the pain. If she is hyper-sensitive to cold temperatures, advise her to take a warm shower.

- **Light Exercise:** Once you have been for a prenatal doctor visit and there are no major concerns from your partner's healthcare provider, it's a good idea for her to begin doing light exercises, like walking. Despite the credibility of her fatigue, remaining completely inactive will only coddle those feelings of tiredness. If you can, take some time out of your day to encourage (not force) your partner to get up and get moving. If she has already been walking, then encourage her to continue doing so. Exercising during the pregnancy will also limit the amount of baby fat she will have to shed after delivery, and her active lifestyle will transfer to the baby, resulting in a healthy, active newborn. If it's sunny out, remind her to use SPF to protect her skin (you probably won't have to), and if you're holding it down in the kitchen, prepare her a high-protein snack at least 30 minutes before the workout so that her blood sugar remains balanced.

WEEK TEN

Your Baby

Now, for the moment you both have been waiting for— your baby is officially a fetus! It's been an arduous journey to get to this point, but every step of the process is important. What's been building up over the past few weeks in terms of the baby's physical attributes will now become more noticeable with baby-like features. Another reason for you and your partner to celebrate is that her gut-wrenching season in the first trimester is finally over now! Although her body will continue to change, the worst part is over … for now.

- **Strawberry Baby:** Remember, just a week ago the embryo upgraded to the size of a green martini olive (it's still no cocktails for your partner). Well, now it has evolved to the size of a strawberry or a prune, roughly measuring 1.2 inches and weighing .14 ounces. Most of this weight is still concentrated toward the head of the fetus, as the brain continues to develop even further, accounting for half of the length of the body at this time. Also, although the baby is still enclosed in the amniotic sac with not much of a view other than the inside of Mommy's belly, the cornea, iris, pupil, lens, and retina are all fully developed to enable his vision. Despite the lack of a view, the eyelids of your fetus will remain closed until your partner is 27 weeks pregnant. By then, baby's limbs will have extended enough to explore their confined territory and, to be honest, look for an exit!

- **Your Baby's Bones Forming:** Speaking of growing limbs, your baby is now beginning to come into their own. Thanks to the massive hormone influx that kept you coping with erratic mood swings and your partner hugging the toilet for a few weeks, your baby is now developing bones and cartilage that are forming small dents along the legs that will later become their knees and ankles. Give it a few more weeks and someone will start soccer practice in the womb. The T-Rex's paddle arms, though not fully matured, are now also flexing with elbows. In every limb of their body, your baby is experiencing exponential growth. But don't call the football coach for a quarterback just yet; these limbs still have much more strength to be built up!

- **First Trimester Ultrasound:** Consider your
  ten-week milestone as graduation for your
  spouse and the baby—from an embryo to a
  fetus. This type of growth calls for an
  ultrasound, which should be the first for the
  entire pregnancy. A significant amount of
  change has happened in the past 10 weeks, and
  now that the embryonic stage is over, the limbs
  and essential organs that have grown should be
  monitored to ensure that there are no defects.
  The first trimester screen is a prime time to
  have genetic testing done, although this is
  optional. One of the more serious tests that will
  be conducted at the 10 to 14-week mark is the
  nuchal translucency screening, more commonly
  referred to as the NT Scan (NTS). Since so
  much attention is being placed on the
  development of the baby's brain, internal
  organs, and external features during this time,
  the NT Scan tests the fetus primarily for the
  risk of Down syndrome and other
  developmental abnormalities. The test includes
  the measurement of your baby's nuchal fold, or
  the back of the neck, for any noticeable
  abnormalities using an ultrasound.
  Additionally, as part of the first trimester
  screen, a fetal DNA test, also known as a Non-

Invasive Prenatal Test (NIPT) will be done when mom's blood is drawn and will screen for Down syndrome, Edwards syndrome, Patau syndrome, and other chromosomal abnormalities. One reason why it is beneficial to perform a genetic test, even though it is optional, is because it screens for chromosomal abnormalities based on family history and genetics. Based on the results of genetic testing, the healthcare provider will know if more invasive tests need to be done, such as the CVS and amniocentesis diagnostic tests. If your baby is at serious risk, invasive tests involve retrieving a genetic sample from within your partner's body, directly from the fetus (*10 Weeks Pregnant*, 2022).

Symptoms to Expect at Week 10

- **Baby Bulges Begin:** Even if you notice it first, don't be the one to point out the slight pudge around her belly. Your partner will more than likely be feeling the effects of the added weight this past week and may begin checking herself out in the mirror. This is where she could be witnessing a slightly rounder abdomen and the beginning of a bulging belly. If this is her first pregnancy, those physical changes may be apparent much sooner. The extent of how soon the baby's growth is visible will also depend on her height and body mass prior to the pregnancy and her fitness level. Do your best to encourage her not to feel unattractive right now. Rather, tell her that she should begin to wear her belly with a sense of pride, knowing that she is carrying a living, growing human being that will someday soon be welcomed into this world to do something amazing. For now, it's merely the size of a grapefruit. So, if the two of you haven't planned on telling anyone of the pregnancy yet, there is still time to cover up!

- **Cancelling Constipation:** As if the constant upset of morning sickness wasn't burdensome enough during the first trimester, constipation just adds on another layer of discomfort. Similar to other symptoms like excess saliva, bloating, mood swings, fatigue, and uncontrollable cravings that present themselves frequently in the first trimester, constipation can also be a recurring thorn in her side. How can you prevent your partner from being clogged up? A few of the foods causing constipation can be white bread, white rice, white flour, pasta, and other densely starchy foods—all things she needs to stay clear of. Instead, you'll want to fill her plate with all sorts of fresh fruits like kiwis, mangoes, apricots, pears, apples, blueberries, strawberries, bananas, and every other fruit you can get your hands on that's not too acidic. Mangoes and bananas, in particular, are not only naturally sweet, but they're also high in potassium and can help with nausea (WhattoExpect, 2021b). Another excellent source of fiber that'll loosen up any blockages with your partner would be whole grains, fiber-rich cereals, nuts, and seeds. The latter also proves to be a great source of natural fats, which play a pivotal role in the cognitive and eye development of the baby. Added to the list are raw or lightly steamed vegetables, especially the dark green leafy ones like kale, spinach, and broccoli. And if, for whatever reason, she is resistant to eating raw fruit or vegetables (food aversion), you can blend your own concoction of vegetables, fruits, and seeds! Add in a little sweetener and she will never know that carrots and cabbage could taste so good in a smoothie.

- **Bane Veins:** Along with the countless changes your partner is experiencing, there may be a sudden appearance of striking, blue veins may across her chest, breasts, and belly. No need to be alarmed though, her mood swings aren't turning her into the Hulk! It's simply a reaction in her body to the increase in blood that's being produced to support her and the baby, especially in the first trimester when the most vigorous growth spurts are underway. She may also start seeing varicose veins in her legs and lower body, which could freak her out, as the sight of them is associated with people of a particular age bracket. Remember that she's now pumping enough blood to support both herself and the baby, and her blood volume increased by almost 50%. It's for this reason that her veins need to be change to keep up with blood flow. The good news, however, is that they often disappear after she gives birth (Marple, 2021a).

WEEK ELEVEN

Your Baby

At close to 3 months into the pregnancy, your baby has grown more distinctly human features since last week. Now that you're past the grueling period of the first trimester, the once-faceless fetus will begin to have more outstanding human characteristics, such as some peach fuzz hair follicles on their crown and on other areas of the body.

As their body begins to stretch and straighten out during this period, their amphibious, webbed-like hands and feet are also growing longer and more separated, with noticeable fingers and toes. And what do babies do when they learn something new? With a fresh set of growing fingers and toes, plus hands and feet that are extending more every week, mom can expect some lunges and practice kicks. Let's take a dive into what the little one is doing down there this week and highlight some of the changes that can be anticipated.

- **Fingers, Toes, and Much More:** In case you're wondering how much your little fighter has grown, baby is approximately 2 inches long, which is about the size of a small fig. The fact that the baby's head still accounts for more than half of their body hasn't changed. However, a few unmistakable differences include the formation of the fingers and toes and a more refined shape of the eyes, nose, mouth, and ears. The growth of the fingers and toes sets the stage for fingernails and toenails, which will begin growing in the upcoming weeks. The good news doesn't stop there, though! It won't be long now before you'll be able to decide whether to decorate the baby shower in pink or blue. By the end of week eleven, the baby's external sex organs will start developing. However, it will be several more weeks before a clear difference can be made between a penis and scrotum in your baby boy or a clitoris and labia in your baby girl. By the next ultrasound, there will be enough development in these areas to tell the difference.

- **Vital Organs:** At eleven weeks, your baby is getting a complete upgrade, from their facial features and limbs to their internal organs. Speaking of which, many of your baby's vital organs are now in place and have been activated to function as they should, such as the liver, kidneys, and pancreas as well as all four chambers of your baby's heart. During your next ultrasound, you should be able to hear the first signs of breathing movements as the nasal passage has now been opened with the completion of the nose (Gates, 2022).

Symptoms to Expect at Week 11

- **Gas and Bloating:** While Mom's appetite and cravings have been through the roof in recent weeks, her hormones could now be up to something a bit more … gassy. That's right! Mom's hormonal changes could begin slowing down her digestion, which can cause constipation, bloating, and gas. The release of progesterone is the main cause of this less-enjoyable side effect. Although its effectiveness in helping develop the baby and maintain a healthy pregnancy is unmatched, part of its function is to relax the muscle tissue in the body, which includes the gastrointestinal tract. This, in turn, slows digestion which allows the nutrients from food to be absorbed into the bloodstream and transferred to the baby. But the constipation and bloating bits are exactly why you should want to be pumping her full of fiber-rich foods to ease her bowels. The more her uterus grows, the more it crowds the stomach and puts added pressure on the digestive tract. To decrease the discomfort of gas and bloating, chef it up in the kitchen with less fried foods and more baked, boiled, or roasted dishes. Also, steer clear of beans, sodas, and sweets as these are guaranteed to cause a spike in gas.

- **A Possible Reprieve:** Despite all the many drastic physical changes, there is light at the end of the first-trimester tunnel, which will officially draw to a close at the end of week twelve. With most women, the heavy foundational work in transforming the embryo into a fetus is over; for the most part, the annoyance of morning sickness and food aversions come to a close at the end of the first trimester. Though your partner's appetite and cravings will fluctuate throughout the remainder of her pregnancy, the most taxing part is over for her … until the time of delivery, that is (WhattoExpect, 2014c).

WEEK TWELVE: THE END OF THE FIRST TRIMESTER

There's no turning back now! You and your partner have officially made it to the end of the first trimester. Don't be fooled, Dad, the baby, and your spouse's tummy haven't been the only things that have been growing. You also grew in character under the weight of all the responsibility you've had to shoulder over the last three months. It was the former Prime Minister of the United Kingdom, Winston Churchill, who said, "You can measure a man's character by the choices he makes under pressure," and if you have made it this far, then your value has already gone up!

Your Baby

At the end of three months, your baby is now the size of a lime, or roughly 2.25 inches in length. That's more than double in size from three weeks ago. That may be hard to imagine, given that there hasn't been much significant change in your partner's outward appearance. But even that is about to change! Another significant aspect of the twelve-week mark that makes it such a milestone is that the possibility of miscarriage is greatly decreased. Usually, from the moment the baby's heartbeat can be heard during the ultrasound, it's a good indication that your spouse has passed the danger zone with your child.

- **All Baby's Vital Organs Are Working:** Once all the tests have checked positive for the first trimester ultrasound, the baby is now fully formed and functional. From here on out, the task will be to maintain the growth of those vital organs over the next 28 weeks (6 months). As you can now understand, everything worked in sync. The first trimester was so brutal for your spouse because the organs and basic framework of the baby were being laid. Now that the organs are in place, most of them already functioning, the intensity of the symptoms has also been reduced. Now, all that is left is for the continued development of the fetus throughout the remainder of her pregnancy.

- **The Heartbeat of Life:** One of the most satisfying sounds you could hear in a lifetime as a father is that of your baby's heart beating for the first time. During your prenatal doctor visit, you will be given the chance to hear your baby's heartbeat as all four walls of the heart are now fully established and will continue developing along with the other organs.

Symptoms to Expect at Week 12

As I alluded to in the previous week's symptoms, quite a few pregnancy symptoms will remain throughout the pregnancy, with some months being more intense than others. A few of the most common recurring symptoms your spouse will be encountering are headaches, food aversions (which may lessen after the first trimester), extreme fatigue (this may be reduced after the first trimester), and tender breasts and nipples. Many of these symptoms will be diminished at this time.

- **Shifting Uterus:** One of the newer occurrences within your partner's body is the migration of her uterus, which is now the size of a grapefruit, from the bottom of her pelvis to the center of her abdomen. The pressure placed on her abdomen and the digestive system can contribute to the dreaded feelings of gas and bloating. However, in special cases, the shifting of the uterus can mean the end of the woman's constant need to urinate.

- **Dizziness:** Another symptom that she will begin encountering from the end of the first trimester and into the beginning of the second trimester is dizzy spells. The progesterone hormone is again the culprit here, and here is why. Similar to the way progesterone slows down mom's digestion ensuring the nutrients enter the bloodstream so that the baby is properly nourished but leaves her with gas, it can make her dizzy. Progesterone causes her blood vessels to relax and expand, which increases the blood flow to the baby. However, it also slows down the blood that returns to mom, resulting in lower blood pressure and decreased blood flow throughout the body and the brain. A lack of blood and oxygen to the brain leads to dizzy spells and feeling faint. Here's a reason for mom's dizziness that doesn't involve progesterone: food. It's extremely important to ensure that your partner is receiving enough food during her pregnancy.

Food helps to regulate her blood sugar, and with too little food, comes low blood pressure, which can leave her feeling dizzy (Gates, 2022). To avoid the attack of dizzy spells, ensure your spouse eats a balanced diet. If she was prone to low blood sugar levels prior to the pregnancy, encourage her to snack on smaller meals or fruit throughout the day to keep her blood sugar level balanced. In the event that she faints or feels dizzy, she should loosen any tight-fitting clothes she is wearing, lie down or sit with her head between her knees, and take deep breaths in and out. This should cause her to feel much better, and once she does, having a snack and something to drink will be a good follow-up.

WAYS TO MAKE YOUR PARTNER FEEL SECURE

There's no better time to make your person feel special and beautiful than during pregnancy. At twelve weeks, she has just begun to see the first signs of a baby bump. You are both probably feeling proud and may even be looking forward to the growth of her tummy. But as excited as she may be, being conscious of her physical appearance is something your partner can't ignore. Don't freak out! There are ways to boost her confidence naturally. How, you may wonder? Let me explain.

- **Boost Her Self Esteem:** A genuine compliment is usually one of the easiest ways of getting a woman to smile and feel validated. If this is something you've been doing throughout the relationship, don't stop now! You partner needs to be reassured that she is beautiful, as she is likely to be feeling insecure about her body with the changes it is going through. So, remind her of how your heart skips a beat when she flashes you that piercing gaze, and have her feeling on top of the world in no time.
- **Be Her Source of Strength:** Words are so empowering. They say, "Sticks and stones may break my bones, but words can never hurt me," but that's not exactly true. Your wife or partner may be feeling overwhelmed, weak, anxious, and afraid during her pregnancy, especially if it's her first child. Of course, her body will feel weak because she is now living for herself and another human being inside of her, but her emotions may be all over the place. Reminding her of how strong, brave, and phenomenal a woman she is to have even made it this far will reinvigorate and strengthen her once again.

- **Bring Her Sexy Back:** Pregnancy will undoubtedly transform your spouse's physical appearance, but it doesn't mean that she gets a one-way ticket to "granny-ville." She still wants to and deserves to feel sexy. Tell her how sexy she is and that she sports the pregnancy like no other woman can. Take it a step further and get her some lingerie. This will take her mind off feeling insecure and back on to keeping things spicy for you in the bedroom!

- **Take Her Out:** This is meant to be a time of growth, joy, expectation, and celebration. So, celebrate this moment of pregnancy by taking your partner out to dinner or for a walk in the city. Maybe take her shopping for maternity wear or get a head start on selecting baby clothes. It's good to keep her moving and not stuck in the house. Plus, you'll be showing her off to the world, proudly and shamelessly, with her lovely belly bump, which will make her feel cherished and confident.

- **Be Involved—Accompany Her to the Doctor:** Part of supporting your spouse involves not only being there for her emotionally but also physically. Accompanying her to doctor visits shows your investment in her and the baby on a deeper level. Also, your presence can make a huge difference in case she receives bad news or must undergo an uncomfortable test. The expected number of scheduled visits for an entire pregnancy is 15 prenatal visits. This is usually broken down into once a month until 28 weeks, then three to four times until week 36. At that point, she will likely go once a week for the last month. From the very first prenatal visit, if you can make a special effort to attend, your spouse will appreciate your presence, and it gives you a chance to ask the physician the questions that'll keep you in the know. Even though your partner is the one carrying the baby, it shouldn't be left entirely up to her to remember every bit of information the doctor gives. Also, the questions you may remember to ask, your partner might forget. That's the power of true partnership. You can inquire from the doctor about what your partner can and cannot do around the house and the best ways you can assist. When you attend a visit, keep a listening ear for the results of her vital signs as the pregnancy progresses, as it will inform you of what foods to avoid when meal prepping and warn you of the symptoms to be expected in that trimester. Besides, you and your partner will be the first to get a glimpse of the growth of the baby at every incremental stage of the growth process. You can start being proud of your little star way before they even make an entrance into the world! Besides doctor's appointments, dads can also accompany their partners to birthing classes. You will need to know the specifics of how your spouse plans on conducting her birth experience, such as who she wants to be present in the room, what type of labor she intends to have (home-birth or traditional hospital labor), what your role will be, and the particular signs to look for, such as labor pain contractions (Downs & MPH, 2009).

- **Keep the Bedroom Active:** Despite the periodical low sex drive, your spouse's hormones can be raging at times, and her body will be calling for attention. You shouldn't be reluctant now but instead, seduce her even more to show that your desire for her is still strong. She's not expecting to go nine months without sex, and neither should you. Make the most of the pregnancy and give her the most unforgettable pregnancy sex ever. Don't be surprised if she is anticipating another baby soon after (Montgomery, 2017)!

There are other things you can do to make your partner feel special during this physical transition, including being mindful of the words you speak, flirting with her in public, being present with her in each moment, and not being phased by the less attractive parts of pregnancy.

You are already aware of what it takes to be committed to helping your spouse. You may have detached from the club life with your friends on a weekend to spend that quality time bonding with your partner and the baby. Or maybe you have been abstaining from any form of alcohol so that you can be fresh every morning to wake up and prepare a nutritious breakfast for your morning-sick spouse. Maybe you decided to stop smoking so that the environment can be free from harmful toxins that will not only be detrimental you, but also to your partner and coming child. By abstaining from certain negative habitual patterns, you will begin to prioritize more meaningful activities, like accompanying your spouse on her doctor visits.

It's also a good point to note that joint parenting, especially if you two are together and plan on keeping it that way, begins long before the actual birth of your baby. Parents need to collaborate and share the responsibility together, even though the woman is the one who is going full term with the pregnancy. Take the initiative without being told what to do, like taking out the garbage, for example, or doing the dishes, as you understand this responsibility is solely on you for only a set period of time.

SAVING FOR LABOR DAY AND BEYOND

Now that you're one week closer to the due date (and approximately 6 months away), it's time to start planning financially for your new home addition. As a new father, you want to think long-term. Every penny should be spent with tomorrow in mind because, let's face it—you're no longer living for yourself. Every decision must be made with your family in mind. But before we get into educational savings accounts and college tuition, let's focus on a few of the immediate costs, pre- and post-pregnancy. The first of those being baby supplies.

- **Supplies:** Almost every doctor will agree that for a newborn baby, breast milk is best. It's an uncontested fact that not only does your newborn receive the best in vitamins and minerals directly from mom's breast milk, but there is also an unspeakable bond that is created between a baby and their mother that helps form a nurturing relationship. However, that doesn't mean that one should completely abandon milk formula. It's safe to assume that for at least the first six months, your baby will drink nothing but milk. The average baby will drink $35 worth of formula per week, although this is subject to change due to recent price increases globally. For one year, that's already close to $2,000. Add in jars of pureed baby food after the six-month mark, and you're looking at another $1,000 or more. Consider that a price tag of $2,500-$3,000 for the first year in food, alone! It's best to encourage your spouse to breastfeed for as long as possible. To save time and money, you can invest in a breast pump to maximize your partner's milk harvest and store away more milk by freezing for the future. This is a wise investment as a breast pump only costs no more than $300, which is much less than $3,000 on formula (Smith, 2019).

- **Nursery Supplies:** Often, your baby won't be coming home to share the bed with their parents—not yet at least. So, the other bit of expense will be the at-home nursery set-up where your newborn will be sleeping and spending time and where you will be changing diapers. These items are essential, so setting aside the funds to purchase them is very important. You'll be needing the following for a basic nursery set-up:

1. It's wise to invest in a dresser for the baby's clothes, diapers, wipes, and other accessories, which will cost another $90-$650, again depending on durability and quality.
2. Along with the dresser, you will also want a changing table specific for those diaper duties. It makes sense to pair that with a convertible changing pad as well, which in total can cost you from $200-$1,100.
3. The last item that is more of an option than a necessity is a rocking chair. It serves as a way for getting babies to fall asleep after their feeding. However, a rocking chair can be seen as a long-term investment for future generations and therefore spend-worthy. To balance the cost, you might want to consider spending less on a crib and dresser, unless you and your partner plan on making another baby in the near future. In any case, it'll cost you between $100 and $500 if you plan on getting one.

- **At-Home Baby Gear:** Depending on where you live and how much walking you and your partner do daily, voluntarily or involuntarily, a durable stroller is something you should invest in. On days when you both feel antsy and decide to take your newborn out for an adventure-filled stroll, you never know what type of terrain you will encounter, so a high-quality stroller is preferred, which can be upward of $100 up to $800. A few other items you may also consider for a max price of $1700 include:

1. car seat
2. playpen/crib
3. baby Carrier
4. bouncer seat
5. baby monitor
6. highchair
7. diaper bag
8. baby gate

- **Diapers, Wipes, and Supplies:** When shopping, you want to get the most bang for your buck. The most effective way to do that is by killing two birds with one stone. For example, when searching for a stroller, choose one that can easily transform into a highchair whenever you go to a restaurant. Some baby bags come already equipped with changing pads and wipes, so you and your partner will have a head start in getting certain things. The sheer necessity of items like diapers, wipes, baby powder, baby soap, and petroleum jelly means there will be the constant use of these items on a daily basis. It's estimated that newborns can use up to 320 diapers per month. That sounds like a lot of trips to the store! To save money, buying diapers and wipes in bulk and online is your best bet. For example, an online order at Amazon can get you 132 Pampers brand diapers for under $40. An average single Pampers brand diaper is about $0.25, costing you $84 per month, which is more than double what you will pay for an online deal. The same can be said for wipes, since there are also deals for the bulk purchase of these as well.

- **Baby Clothes:** Baby clothes also include the maternity clothes that you and mom had to invest in once her belly bump started showing as a result of the baby's growth. But regarding clothes specific to your newborn, you may want to invest in a variety of the following:

1. sleepers
2. onesies
3. hats
4. socks
5. gowns
6. clothing for hot and cold temperatures
7. coats
8. pants and tops

Each of these items has a price tag of $2–$25 per piece of clothing. Keep in mind as well that your baby will be growing dramatically henceforth, so buying clothing in advance from 0-3 months to 3-6 months and 6-9 months to 9-12 months and so on is a wise way of thinking ahead. You save money by buying these items in multiples when they're out of season, that way they'll cost much less than when the season approaches. However, this is reserved for more of a mom's choice, who is always on the lookout for sales on cute items to dress up her little prince or princess in. Regardless of who enjoys playing dress-up with their children more, it will be beneficial to buy the clothes a few sizes bigger to be used later down the road. In total, baby clothes can run you a rough estimate price of $1,000.00.

- **Long-Term Savings:** Now that we've covered the more immediate expenses for pre- and post-pregnancy, it's time to look a bit further into the future. Depending on your socioeconomic class (upper, middle, or lower), you will need to determine how much you can save for your child's future and which financial plans you'd be able to afford as a new parent. This can include healthcare insurance, life insurance, educational savings plans, and such. Let's look at some of the best and smartest ways to get started on your child's future.

1. Health Insurance

If you already have yourself on a health insurance plan, that's a great start. A health insurance plan costs an average of $400 per month for an added dependent. Of course, you will want to discuss your health plan options with an agent to find which is most cost-effective and beneficial to you and your child. Most health insurance providers consider having a baby a qualifying life event, which enables you to make changes to your health policy or enroll in a new one altogether. If you decide to do so, most health insurance providers require that your child be added to your plan within 30 or 60 days post-delivery.

2. Life Insurance

Life insurance is an investment that if you

haven't looked into yet, you should seriously consider. Not only can it be used as collateral in taking home loans, student loans, or mortgages, but it is also advised if you have anyone in your life that's dependent on you financially, whether that be a child, a spouse, or anyone else. By going online or speaking with a life insurance provider, you can determine how much life insurance you need to buy, the number of years you want to support, and whether you want to include coverage of pricey items like a mortgage or college loans.

As a "Virgin Dad," this is definitely something you want to look into to safeguard your family financially in the event of any worst-case scenarios, like death. And the younger you start, the better. If you begin as a 30-year-old pursuing a 20-year-term life insurance policy of $500,000, payments start as low as $30 per month. If you're 40-years-old and seeking the same term insurance, it will be between $30-$40 a month, and the monthly premium increases with age.

3. Long-Term Disability Insurance

Life insurance is undoubtedly the most common form of insurance people choose, especially parents with spouses and children as dependents. But another type of insurance that is also a viable option is long-term disability insurance. While death is the ultimate worst-case scenario that can happen to release your insurance benefits to your family, life isn't always so cut-and-dry, and there are other unfortunate things that can occur before death, such as sickness or critical injury. This is especially for you, dad, if you work in a construction job, a warehouse job, as a fireman, a policeman, or any other physically demanding occupation that puts you at risk. Basically, disability insurance pays you a percentage of your income for the specified time. Disability insurance can be long-term or short-term and is usually offered by your employer or by a private insurance provider.

4. An Emergency Fund

Despite having insurance, it shouldn't be viewed as a source of emergency funding in the event of the unexpected, like job loss. If there is anything we should have learned from the COVID-19 pandemic, it is that nothing is secure. Your entire life and career can be plunged into uncertainty overnight with no sign of reprieve in sight. Such was the case for many families where there was a sole breadwinner. It's for this reason that having an emergency fund in place to cover basic home expenses and necessities for at least 6 months to a year (or longer depending on your budget) is vital. If you have been laid off or are even thinking of changing careers, a backup fund will be able to sustain you and your family until you are settled.

5. Creating a Will

As a good father-to-be, nothing will bring you more comfort than knowing that if you were to depart this world, your children and family would be taken care of. And since none of us knows our predestined date of death, it's important to get a will made with beneficiaries named on your accounts for the peaceful dispersion of your assets. If you have already planned for your retirement with a 401K, the possibility of your untimely passing can leave your loved ones fighting over the funds left behind. A will can be done for $400, although more complex versions can cost between $1,000 and $3,500. It will be worth it to ensure that your family is taken care of after your passing. When doing your will, you may also want to speak with your parents, an aunt, uncle, cousin, or close friend about being a separate guardian of the state who will delegate the accounts until your children reach adulthood.

6. Saving for Your Child's College Tuition

One of the most important things to get ahead in life nowadays, is an education. The only other financial security for your child besides placing them as beneficiaries on your life insurance is equipping them with an education to be able to fend for themselves in the world. If you are a forward-thinking father, you will want your child to exceed your expectations and even surpass you in this life. Therefore, saving for their education now will place them at an advantage later on.

College tuition has doubled over the past 3 decades, and from the looks of things, it's only expected to increase. Luckily, there are plans such as the 529 plan, which provides a tax advantage that can be used only for qualified educational expenses. Although the 529 plan has been traditionally used for college, it has since been altered to be used for qualified expenses at earlier stages in your child's life, such as a private K-12 education (Berry-Johnson, 2018).

RED FLAGS DURING FIRST TRIMESTER

By now, you're aware that while pregnancy is a joyous time for the celebration of life, it is also a serious and sensitive time, especially for your partner. There are many internal complications that can go wrong during the first trimester, as this is a time when a woman's body is being put under immense pressure to form the embryo once implantation begins. Some of these symptoms are actually common for a newly pregnant woman. Where it becomes a danger is when the symptoms last longer than normal or when certain pains seem unusually extreme, such as excessive nausea and excruciating cramps. Here are some of the signs that indicate your partner is not having a normal pregnancy (Mann, 2022).

- vaginal bleeding
- excessive nausea
- high fever
- abdominal pain
- vaginal discharge/dark urine
- pain during urination
- leg pain/severe headaches
- flare up of pre-existing diseases

If any of these symptoms appear during the first trimester of your partner's pregnancy and last, contact her healthcare provider immediately. Trying to wait it out in hopes that the symptoms go away is not only irresponsible but can also lead to fatality depending on the severity of the symptom (Johnson, 2017).

☆ HOME IS WHERE THE HEART BEATS: A PERSONAL STORY

I've endured grueling training as an amateur boxer, suffered a broken arm in a car accident, and have even been mugged at gunpoint, and I can truly say that none of these events could have prepared me for the first few months of my wife's pregnancy. I know it sounds dramatic, but it requires a different level of mental toughness and emotional intelligence to deal with a pregnant woman. From the unpredictable mood swings to not being able to fry an egg without her puking all over the toilet bowl, it was an experience I honestly wouldn't be able to forget even if I tried. I can sincerely say that I've been humbled.

Despite the roles being switched temporarily, where I became the home cook (I learned from YouTube videos) and was tasked with keeping the entire house clean, I would do it all over again for my wife. It was an honor for me to cater to her needs because, after all, she is carrying our future son. And yes, I said son, even though it won't be another few months before we can confirm what the baby's sex is—I'm calling first dibs!

There we were, on the last leg of the first trimester. "So, how have the two of you been coping with the pregnancy thus far? This is your first child, correct?" asked

Dr. Longh, a middle-aged Cuban doctor who ran a small private health care facility with his petite wife, Isabela. He glanced over at me as if to signal that the question was for me to answer.

"Well …" I began, "It's been a different experience for sure. I've been doing my best to keep up with the symptoms she's been experiencing. I also requested some time off from work so I can stay home and look after her. And to answer your question: Yes…This will be our first child," I responded calmly.

Dr. Longh continued to probe, this time directing his questions to my wife, "Have you been experiencing any unusual symptoms during this time? Like prolonged feelings of nausea or unbearable abdominal cramps?"

"No," my wife replied. "I mean … I've been experiencing cramps and fatigue and morning sickness, but I wouldn't say that it's been out-of-the-ordinary. I also realize that I have a newfound hatred for the smell of raw eggs … but that's about it," she concluded, with a slightly concerned look on her face. "Oh, and how can I forget?! This man has been taking care of me very well! I've been getting back rubs, foot rubs … rubs everywhere!" she exclaimed while staring at me with excitement.

"Hahaha!" Dr. Longh chuckled. "Well, it seems you've been doing your duties, sir," he said, flashing a wink at me. "But you don't have to worry. All this hard work … will not be in vain. Because now you get to hear your baby's heartbeat!" he said, smiling at me.

He had my wife lay down and applied the ultrasound gel to her lower abdomen. Then Dr. Longh placed the transducer probe in the same area and began to gently press down onto her tummy while simultaneously looking at the display on the computer monitor.

"Aaah … There we go. Here is your bebe bonita." he said ecstatically. "Listen close," he urged me, signaling me to come closer. "You hear that?"

I moved closer to the screen, trying to make sense of the black and white blur I was seeing. Then, I heard a heavy, rapid rhythm. It became steady but kept the same fast-paced rhythm. It was my child's heartbeat! I looked at my wife and managed to flash a reassuring smile, although I was struggling to come to grips with reality in my own mind. "This is really happening," I whispered to myself. All the symptoms of morning sickness, fatigue, and mood swings couldn't replace the evidence I was now met with. I was actually hearing the heartbeat of a human being built as an extension of myself.

Before now, I hadn't seen the need to attend every single doctor's visit. I thought she would just be able to ask her mother or sister to accompany her for those in the future. But I realized, from that moment, that I didn't have to wait for our child to be born to start making him feel the love and support from both of us. That feeling of love and acceptance had to be cultivated right now. So, regardless of my workload, I endeavored to be present at every doctor's appointment to support my wife and our baby. It was the least I could do, being that she was the one carrying around the extra weight of a new life, literally!

QUESTIONS AND ANSWERS: WHAT FATHERS NEED TO KNOW

Questions:

1. Should my partner be exercising? If so, how much?
2. Is it normal to be nervous about her changing body?
3. Am I a jerk if I am mourning the loss of my old life?

Answers:

1. Yes. Your partner should aim to establish good habits during her pregnancy to remain active. She can engage in light exercises like walking, swimming, and water aerobics, although more vigorous exercises like jogging, running, and moderate weightlifting are also acceptable during the first trimester. Workouts should last between 10-20 minutes per session.

2. Every man has a different perspective of their wife or girlfriend during pregnancy. Most men find their partners adorable and are even more attracted to them, while others can't stomach the idea of being sexually intimate with a baby between them. So, it all depends on the way you respond to her changing body.

3. It's totally normal to miss your child-free life prior to being a dad-to-be. Both fathers and mothers often reminisce on the freedom they once had before taking up such a major responsibility. Getting into a routine, knowing your role and responsibility as a father, and integrating the baby into your life are some ways to cope with parenthood. However, being a parent doesn't mean that your life is over. You can still find the time to do things by yourself

and even hang with friends every now and
then.

The end of week twelve and the beginning of week
thirteen signify a threshold that has been crossed. Your
baby is growing more mature in the womb and has
reached the stage of a fetus, so you can expect even
greater changes this coming week and beyond. Before
you know it, you and your spouse will be holding your
lovable, kicking, and screaming bundle of joy!

4

DID YOU SAY YOU'RE HORNY?— THE FOURTH MONTH

"Stop saying, 'We're pregnant.' You're not pregnant! Do you have to squeeze a watermelon-sized person out of your lady-hole? No. Are you crying alone in your car listening to a stupid Bette Midler song? No. When you wake up and throw up, is it because you're nurturing a human life? No. It's because you had too many shots of tequila." If you've ever seen the movie *Bad Moms*, then you'll know that this passionate rant, delivered ever-so eloquently by Mila Kunis, can be seen as the heart cry for every mother who has gone through or is currently going through the turbulence of pregnancy.

WEEK THIRTEEN

You are past the first quarter of the pregnancy! You've overcome a lot together as a couple, and the greatest thing to take out of it is that your bond will become much stronger. If you and your partner have decided to keep the pregnancy a secret up until now, you may want to begin letting the cat out of the bag at this time, especially since the beginnings of a baby bump is beginning to show itself. But there's no pressure to do so. If you prefer to let friends and family find out on their own regularly, then that's perfectly fine!

Your Baby

So, exactly how big is a peapod? It's somewhere around 2.64 inches from crown-to-rump in length. While the baby's features are definitely more noticeable, it's not fully matured physically and may still appear creature-like. Don't be worried that your baby isn't growing fast enough or that they will be stunted like this forever. Every baby grows at a different pace, which dictates how fast or slow the developmental process will be.

- **Forming Teeth and Bones:** With the foundation of a skeletal outline and the organs in place, your baby's nimble bones are now beginning to harden in their arms, legs, and skull. They may be able to fidget a bit more at this time, something that will become more pronounced as the weeks wear on. And while it'll be months before baby will be able to use them, they're also becoming denser, like the rest of the bones in their body.

- **Vocal Cord:** Your baby's vocal cords are developing even further this week, but don't get curious and purchase a stethoscope in hopes of hearing early coos from inside the womb. That's wishful thinking! You'll have to wait until after the water bag bursts and your baby breathes their first breath out in the real world before you will be able to hear the freedom cry! Until then, your future vocalist will remain in hibernation mode, working on their craft.

- **Intestinal Changes:** On the other hand, there's been a lot of change in your baby's intestines. They have recently shifted from being conjoined with the umbilical cord to now finding a permanent home in your baby's abdomen. As the fetus continues to grow, the placenta grows alongside it to ensure it grows healthily. A good sign that the baby's intestines are now working independently of the umbilical cord is the fact that it has begun excreting its own urine and feces, produced from swallowing amniotic fluid. The amniotic fluid that has built up in your baby will produce meconium, which will be their first fecal matter (Gates, 2021).

Symptoms to Expect at Week 13

Besides a possible pause in morning sickness, she may also be experiencing a few changes.

- **A Return to Normalcy:** Luckily for you, in the third month, you can expect your spouse to be acting more like herself with the decreasing influx of hormones. The second trimester isn't quite there yet, but toward the end of the 13th week, there should be marked changes in the symptoms she has been experiencing. However, symptoms don't disappear for all women during this time. For some, nausea and fatigue can spill over into the fourth and fifth months, while for others, the more grievous symptoms, such as bloating, constipation, headaches, and breast tenderness, can fluctuate extremely throughout the entire pregnancy.
- **Vaginal Discharge:** Vaginal discharge is a common symptom among pregnant women, especially leading up to the second trimester. While some of the symptoms mentioned above

may be disappearing for some, an increase in vaginal discharge is likely to occur at this time. Its scientific name is leukorrhea, and it is described as a thin, milky white substance that is either odorless or mildly scented. This discharge will likely increase as the pregnancy progresses and is again caused by the production of estrogen. Its function is to prevent infection in the birth canal as well as maintain a healthy balance of vaginal bacteria. However, the downside is that it leaves its mark on your partner's pants, which your partner will be more than happy to gift you in the laundry room. The only concerns to be aware of regarding leukorrhea will be if the color is gray, yellow, or green; causes pain or other forms of discomfort; or produces a strong, repulsive odor, as this can be indicative of an infection. If these signs appear in your partner, it's best to contact her healthcare provider for a professional opinion (Donaldson-Evans, 2021e).

- **Cramping:** As mentioned earlier, certain symptoms that occurred in the prior weeks may continue into the coming months or may become less frequent now. One of the most common is cramping, which can be caused by other estrogen-induced symptoms like gas and bloating. If your partner's cramping becomes more severe after attempting remedies like a hot shower, ginger tea, consuming more liquids, or simply lying down, then she should contact her midwife, especially if it happens over a prolonged period.

- **Common Symptoms:** If your spouse is still experiencing other common symptoms like digestion problems or outstanding varicose veins, there's no need to be alarmed. The visibility of the varicose veins across her breasts, chest, and belly only suggest that there is an increased blood flow being produced for her and the baby. They usually become less obvious once the baby is born. In the case of heartburn and indigestion, avoid cooking fried, spicy, and acidic foods for your partner. You can also suggest that she try eating smaller meal portions or chewing gum after meals to help balance her stomach acids.

- **Feeling Frisky:** Your spouse's moods may swing you straight into bed at times, especially with the increase in vaginal discharge coupled with the greater rush of blood through her body. If she has gone from a volatile state to asking for it, just go with the flow, because you can end up satisfying her needs more than you know! Plus, you're both probably in the mood for some pregnancy sex to release the tension from the first trimester. I advise you to take it as it comes, dad, because her frisky feelings won't last for long and will probably fluctuate throughout the entire pregnancy. There's also no need to hold back for fear of hurting the baby since your little trooper is protected by her uterus and a wall of muscle. If anything, he'll be enjoying the ride!

WEEK FOURTEEN

You can officially breathe a sigh of relief that you and your partner have made it safely through the first trimester. Like anything else in life, it's been a time of highs and lows, but for most women, this is a period where nausea and fatigue are now fading away. There's more good news involving the baby as well. Let's check out the progress report of your baby genius this week.

Your Baby

- **Baby Is Growing and Standing:** Now that your partner has entered the second trimester, the baby will be growing exponentially and has grown over an inch since the last week, measuring 3.25 to 4 inches long. In layman's terms, he went from a lemon to a full-sized orange, or the size of a clenched fist. The increase in size also brings with it growth in other areas, such as increased movement, hair growth, and more defined facial features. As your potential dancer continues their growth journey, baby's neck is getting stronger which is lending support to their head. This, in turn, enables her to stand up straight, in the amniotic sac at least. The usual slouching posture is being straightened, and the movements are even more intentional, but fluid. As part of their practice, the fetus may also be trying to breathe by inhaling amniotic fluid into and out of its lungs. A closer assessment may also reveal an array of different facial expressions on your baby's face. You are likely to see a frown, a pucker, or even a grin. Now, you'll get to see who your little one takes after the most (Donaldson-Evans, 2021).

- **Hair Growth:** It's not uncommon to see some babies born with a full head of hair. During week 14, you can expect hair to start shooting up on the baby's head as well as on the eyebrows. However, that's not the only area where hair is expected to grow. Mom's amazing biological design has enough intuition to know that the fetus will need to be cozy on those cold winter nights and provides a thin, soft layer of hair known as lanugo, which is there to provide warmth. This thin bed of hair won't be there forever. Once the baby's fat begins to accumulate later in the pregnancy, the lanugo sheds naturally since it has already fulfilled its purpose.

- **The Gender Reveal:** You have both been waiting patiently for it, and the time for a gender reveal is right around the corner. During this week, the baby's external sex organs have been formed. So, dad, you'll finally be able to lay your convictions to rest about the fetus being a boy. The other organs, like the thyroid gland have also begun to make hormones, which can be the reason for the sex organs becoming more pronounced. Your baby's digestive organs are also continuing to produce its first bowel movement, meconium, and the liver is also in the process of making bile. The amazement doesn't stop with your young one.

Symptoms to Expect at Week 14

- **Round Ligament Pain:** In case she hasn't experienced it before, your spouse may be in for a new kind of pain in this second trimester known as round ligament pain. These are sharp, stabbing pregnancy growth pains that occur on one or both sides of the abdomen and usually start around the 14-week period and continue into the second trimester. This is all due to her increasing weight. As the uterus grows, the supporting ligaments that connect her groin to her abdomen begin to stretch in order to accommodate her weight. Each time the weight rests on the ligaments, it causes an achy feeling in the lower abdomen. You can try to ease her pain by elevating her feet and placing her in a restful, comfortable position.
- **Increased Energy and Fewer Bathroom Breaks:** Your partner will be ecstatic to know that she can breathe much easier now and that she'll be feeling a surge of energy. For most women, the extreme fatigue is over, and they will regain much of the energy that was once missing. Unfortunately, not everyone falls into this bracket, as other women experience worsening feelings of fatigue as the months

progress. So, let's hope your spouse falls into the first category and regains her energetic spirit once again, along with a resurrected sex drive, which you should be happy to cater to. An additional welcome relief comes as a decreased need to urinate. The previous season may have been an annoyance for her—maybe you as well. Decreased morning sickness, less tender breasts, and fewer trips to the bathroom usually go hand in hand, so let's hope she will be one of the lucky ones (Pevzner, 2021c).

WEEK FIFTEEN

Your Baby

- **All About the Baby Look:** It's now week fifteen, and among the good news to be expected, your baby has grown to 6.57 inches, or about the size of a succulent pear. In case you're wondering, this week marks the fourth month of pregnancy for your partner. It's been said since week 7, but now the fetus's face is more evenly proportioned. The ears are properly fitted on either side of the head, and the eyes have moved from the side of the head to the front in a more symmetrical position. To accompany the natural face-lift on your handsome prince or pretty princess are distinct eyelids, eyebrows, eyelashes, nails, hair, fingers, and toes that are defined enough to wiggle about. All that's left now is to give a gender to this darling baby.

- **It Tastes Great:** With the mouth, lips, gums, and jawline being formed during this week, baby's tastebuds are forming and will start connecting to brain receptors. In the next five weeks, the taste buds should be completed, although the only thing they'll be sucking on right now is a thumb. Although their taste buds will soon be producing taste, the food passed through the bloodstream and into the amniotic sac is still tasteless. The good thing is that they're getting the essential nutrients necessary for further growth and aren't able to tell you they hate broccoli—yet.

- **Baby's Practice Movements:** The growth of facial features, organs, and taste buds has also filtered out to the other limbs of the major body parts, such as the arms and legs. Your little league pitcher may not be making big dents in Mom's tummy as yet, but that doesn't mean they aren't busy working. Baby's legs have grown longer than their arms, and their limbs are fully functional, giving them a chance to flex those muscles and get busy. Your little munchkin has also been practicing breathing exercises—breathing, sucking, and swallowing —so that they won't be a fish out of water when he leaves the aquarium (amniotic sac) (Donaldson-Evans, 2021f). Neither of you may be able to feel it just yet, but your baby is kicking and punching like a mini-Bruce Lee. But he's not planning to *Enter the Dragon*. For now, he's preparing to enter the world, and this behavior will continue in the coming weeks to the point where you will be feeling those kicks and punches for yourself, while your wife copes with the never-ending activity.

Symptoms to Expect at 15 Weeks

- **Swollen and Bleeding Gums:** It seems like when one abhorrent symptom lets up, another one begins. Your spouse, if she was fortunate enough, probably just began to enjoy a reprieve from the constant gagging of morning sickness. Now, something else is on the horizon, and this time it's not coming from her gut, but it's in her mouth. Once again, those hormones are back at it. As good as they are for the development of the baby, your spouse's hormones tend to get her into quite a bit of trouble. Her pregnancy hormones are now being used to cause infections like gingivitis, which result in the inflammation of the gums. Pregnancy gingivitis is not her fault as it wasn't a lack of hygiene that triggered it. But what she can do is continue practicing good oral hygiene by flossing daily, brushing gently two to three times a day, and possibly scheduling a dental appointment for the removal of any excess plaque, as the bacterium in plaque is the main cause of gingivitis.

- **Feeling Stuffy in the Nosebleeds?** Her hormones aren't done with the assault just yet. If gingivitis and swollen gums weren't bad enough, the hormones, in addition to increasing blood flow to her mucous membrane, will now be causing her nasal congestion. Like the common cold being called "the flu," nasal congestion is so common during pregnancy that it's been named "rhinitis of pregnancy." Chronic congestion can also lead to something that is equally dreaded: nosebleeds. To get relief from nasal congestion before it leads to this, using a humidifier or vaporizer in the room she sleeps in might help. As an alternative, she can sleep in an elevated position with mounted pillows, flush out her system with plenty of fluids, or use a saline nasal spray. If all else fails and she encounters nosebleeds, they're usually harmless. Although, don't think twice to call her obstetrician, especially if they are frequent or the flow is heavy. If a heavy flow persists for more than 30 minutes, make plans to get her to the emergency room right away.

- **Gaining Weight:** It's only natural that as the baby grows in size, so will mom, right? She should be growing with the chunky monkey inside her stomach. And that's exactly what it will be. Now that her food aversions and nausea have ceased, she can resume eating the foods she loves. No more toilet hugging! During the second trimester, your spouse needs to eat enough to gain a pound a week, or about 340 extra calories a day. And no, that doesn't only mean fatty foods. According to the guidance of her practitioner, the meals you prepare should be nutritionally sound. Examples of nutritional snacks can be apples and cheese, veggies or chips and guacamole, mashed avocado and toasted bread or crackers, waffles with peanut butter and pear, and homemade trail mix (Gates, 2022c). But let's use wisdom here. It's recommended that she gain four pounds a month, which does not mean that you should allow your wife to blow up like a pufferfish. Now that she has regained much of her energy and is no longer plagued with fatigue, you should encourage her with an exercise routine. Or better yet, if you have the time, motivate her by beginning with her. It's easy for her to adopt a slothful attitude and use the pregnancy as an excuse for sitting around all day. An active body and an active mind go together, so you can lovingly suggest that the two of you begin a pregnancy workout routine. Never forget that much of what mom feels, the baby feels also. For lack of a better term, the baby is basically a parasite living off your partner for the duration of the pregnancy. Their dependence on her goes beyond food and includes emotions, attitudes, and behavioral patterns as well. As a father watching their child grow in their mother's womb, you have to set the tone now with your presence. With that said, let's dive right into week 16 and see what new accomplishments your little peanut has achieved over the past week.

WEEK SIXTEEN

Your Baby

- **Baby Is the Size of an Avocado:** Can you believe that what started as an embryo the size of an orange seed has evolved so rapidly to the size of an avocado! Did somebody order guacamole?! That's an impressive amount of growth over a 4-month period. But exactly how big is an avocado? On average, they measure 4 to 5 inches and weigh a little over 5 ounces, which is a considerable amount of growth since last week. Let's take a closer look at what's been going on with Speedy Gonzales inside there.

- **Heart Growing Stronger:** At week 16, there is so much going on with the baby right now, like the fact that the backbone and other back muscles are gaining more strength to be able to support and straighten the neck and head even more. Your unborn child has definitely come a long way from the hunched-over creature it began as. Part of this tremendous growth includes one of the core muscles of every human: the heart. The baby's heart is currently pumping 25 quarts of blood each day, which is exactly 100 cups. And this amount is only expected to increase.

- **Baby Is Sensitive to Light:** Your baby's eyes have been closed and under maintenance for some time now, and they're finally beginning to show signs of life. Due to the development of surrounding interconnecting facial muscles, the baby's eyes move from side to side under shut eyelids whenever he perceives light. With their eyes sensitive to light, soon he'll also be able to hear mom and dad's voices! At that point, it's good to sing to them or listen to soothing music so they know they're entering a peaceful environment.

Symptoms to Expect at 16 Weeks

- **Back Pain:** The round ligament pain that was mentioned in week 14 may still be present now since it's a second-trimester symptom. But other than that, there are symptoms such as back pain, which is something many women face during pregnancy. One of the causes of back pain is again known to be your spouse's hormonal release, meant to loosen the joints and ligaments that are attached to her spine and pelvic bone. This happens ahead of time to prepare for labor. Another reason for immense back pain is an expanding uterus, which puts extra strain on that area. If, for any of these reasons, your partner is suffering from back pain, offer your partner a massage. Or she can also schedule a prenatal massage with a more professional practitioner.

- **Nasal Congestion Continues:** As it was mentioned earlier in week 15, nasal congestion is an unwanted stress that your partner will have to deal with. And that will be due to two factors: an increase in blood flow and the swelling of the mucus membranes in her nose, both caused by hormones. Sadly, the congestion is expected to worsen as the pregnancy continues and can also result in nosebleeds.

- **Other Possible Symptoms:** With all the highly nutritious food she's been eating recently plus the boost of energy she's been feeling ever since the fatigue has said goodbye, your spouse will be feeling up to some much-needed bedroom activity. The body wants what it wants, and with the added lubrication of leukorrhea, she'll be in the mood for action. But apart from that, your partner's breasts are likely to be experiencing additional changes. Aside from the tenderness, prominent veins, and nipple color change, she can also develop lumps in her breasts. Hold on, though. They're not what you think, if you're thinking of cancer. During pregnancy, milk-filled cysts called galactoceles or breast tumors called fibroadenomas appear in preparation for feeding your newborn post-pregnancy. It's actually rare for a woman to develop cancer during pregnancy.

ANNOUNCING YOUR PREGNANCY

Pregnancy is the only other major news revelation besides marriage that people want to be sure is fool proof before announcing. This is especially true for women who want to avoid the embarrassment of disclosing their pregnancy status too soon, only to find out that there has been a miscarriage. This can not only be embarrassing but extremely heartbreaking, more so for your partner, since she is the one carrying the baby. But there may be strategic ways you or your partner might want to go about revealing the big news.

When Is It Safe to Tell Others?

The end of the first trimester (12 weeks pregnant) is usually the time that doctors consider it "safe" to start telling others of the pregnancy because it's considered "out of the woods" in terms of a miscarriage. If you and your partner have had a history of miscarriages, then waiting until after the 12-week mark will be a good idea, although it's not a rule that's set in stone for others to follow.

Another reason you or your partner may be waiting to tell others is that the marriage was not planned. Perhaps no one will be expecting a pregnancy to come out of your union with your partner. Or perhaps no one even knew there was a union to begin with. Whether planned or unplanned, you each want to deal with your feelings and see where you both stand before making the pregnancy public.

▷ **Employers**

With your partner being pregnant, it's safe for her to continue working unless directed otherwise by your obstetrician. Depending on where she lives, there is also no law requiring her to tell an employer at any specific time that she is pregnant. However, her employment contract will more than likely give directives on how many months or weeks before taking parental leave, she should inform her employer. It's also a good idea for her to tell her employer of the pregnancy personally before hearing it from someone else.

▷ Co-Workers

Whether or not she tells her employer right away, the symptoms will start to show, such as fatigue and morning sickness. Her symptoms will surely affect her work performance, so it's wise to give her employers a heads-up beforehand. Dad can also apply for parental leave and, like expecting mothers, can apply for 12 weeks of unpaid time off after the birth of the child.

▷ Family

If the relationship with your spouse is more solid than that of Seth Rogan and Katherine Heigl in *Knocked Up*, then it's best to plan your pregnancy announcement together. Again, once she has passed the safe period after 12 weeks, the first set of people you'll want to tell is her family. You might want to accompany her in breaking the news to her parents to show your support from the beginning, especially if this is their first grandchild. It'll be a welcome cause for celebration among her family and yours!

▷ Friends

If you and your partner share a common circle of friends who are well aware of your relationship status, then they will be ready to celebrate immediately! But if you want to keep it from being broadcast all over social media, the person you consider a close best friend will be the first to know since your secret will be kept safe, and the same can be said for your spouse.

As the pregnancy becomes undeniable with the growth of your partner's belly, you can both decide to share a picture on social media so that your wider circle of friends is made aware. A subtle post, like that of an ultrasound picture, will speak volumes without having to actually announce the pregnancy.

TAKE HER CLOTHES SHOPPING

It may only be in the beginning stages, but at the end of 16 weeks, your spouse is getting noticeably bigger in waist and taste. She is probably fighting just to fit into the jeans she was once able to slip on effortlessly. And if that's the plight she is faced with, then it's time to take her shopping. Now is the perfect time for her to start fitting into her maternity clothes since she will be gaining weight along with the rapidly growing baby that she is carrying. Experts suggest that between 12 and 18 weeks is the best time to make the switch to comfortable maternity pants, leggings, tops, cardigans, loose-fitting blouses, and sizeable dresses.

Of course, this batch of clothes will consist of casual and work clothes, if she is well enough to go back to work, as not all women have a smooth-sailing pregnancy. Take into account that close to the third trimester, her hormones will begin acting up again in the area of gas and bloating, which means she will be feeling a great deal of discomfort. As a result, her clothes should at least be comfortable. However, keep in mind that maternity clothes can be expensive. So, if you're looking for an opportunity to save, in the next few weeks, a few of your sweatshirts might fit her just fine. If she's around the house, she can throw these on to keep warm. Also, keep in mind that she will be using these new clothes for only 3 to 6 months, so there's no need to buy an excessive amount of clothing. However, there are a few essentials your spouse will need for home and work. Some of these will be:

- stretchy maternity tank tops (for breast changes)
- maternity jeans or pants
- business-casual maternity work pants and skirts
- an oversized blouse or cardigan
- athletic clothing (leggings)
- pregnancy dresses

These are just a few maternity options. But since this is a billion-dollar industry, there are plenty of clothes you and your partner can find on sale or in stores where there are clothes swaps being done. Before going on a shopping spree, you can advise your spouse to check her wardrobe for belted dresses (minus the belt), cardigans, large denim shirts, large button-down blouses, and tunic tops to see how she can incorporate them into her maternity wear.

☆ TUMMY TUM-TUM: A PERSONAL STORY

So, it's about week 16 and, by now, it was becoming apparent that she was packing on some extra weight. I would playfully tease her, which would sometimes end in a terrible turn of mood that left me blindsided and scratching my head, wondering how it went from 0 to 1,000 so quickly. Blame the hormones—at least that's what her doctor told me.

Realizing that none of her work clothes fit and her casual outing clothes were hugging her tighter than a pair of 1970s leather pants, I decided it was time for her to get a few additions to her wardrobe. At least for the pregnancy. Ever since her morning sickness and food aversions gave her a break, she's been pigging out on healthy snacks. By healthy, I mean stuff like yogurt, cheese, grilled chicken breast, vegetable lasagna, and even some ice cream. I was happy for her because I saw firsthand the way she suffered from keeping food down. So, I was happy that she got a break too!

We were preparing to head out for her maternity clothes now. And while I was excited to get out of the house with her, I was ready to get it over with—I'm not the shopping type. Can you find me a man who is?

"Hey, are you ready to go? I don't want to get out there too late … Ladies are having babies nowadays like crazy. So, I hope we'll be able to find something good for you!" I called out to her from the kitchen. We were both getting ready at an even pace, and for some reason, she seemed to hit the pause button after putting on her pants.

"Yea … Ugh … I'm in the bedroom, babe. Almost done … just trying to get … these … pants on!" She yelled in frustration. From where I was standing, it sounded like she was wrestling a wild animal. "See honey, that's why I told you I needed new clothes. I'm blowing up like a balloon that's ready to pop!"

I must admit that she'd been after me since week 12 of the pregnancy to get her some maternity dresses and leggings. But she didn't seem that big to me. Plus, getting time off from work was hard enough. I knew this was the only time I was given a reprieve, so I wanted to get as much done today as possible.

"I know, babe. But you know how hectic it's been at work. I'm trying to do all that needs to be done so there will be no problems when I request paternal leave to be here after the baby is born," I replied, walking toward the bedroom to see just how dire the situation was. When I got inside, I couldn't contain myself. I saw my wife on her back with her feet in the air, struggling to pull a pair of jeans on that she wore with no issue just last week. "Hahaha!! Babe, that's what's been taking you so long? You need to throw those pants in a corner … they can barely go up past your hips," I said jokingly, observing the impossibility of the mission she was on.

"You clown," she replied with a smirk. "Can you help me? Please?! At this point, I'm about to go out in my panties," she said, looking at me in desperation. She had already worked up a sweat trying to put the pants on, and I wondered what else she could put on.

"At this point, you can stay in that position and we can cancel this trip. I'm in love with the shape of you!" I flirted. In recent weeks, she'd really been in the mood, and it got my fire burning. Now, I was always ready to spark a fire!

"Hmmm...That sounds like a good idea," she stopped and smiled seductively at me. "Don't start something you can't finish, misterrr," she teased jokingly, spreading her arms open to receive me. I embraced her, and we kissed passionately for a few seconds before…

"Babe, we need to get you these clothes," I said, not wanting to get carried away. "You know what? I have an idea!"

"Hey now … you got me going and now you wanna stop?" Her face pouted. "Don't play with me like that." She countered, throwing the tight-fitting jeans at me.

"If we're having a girl, I hope she makes the same face as you when she gets mad. She will look cute just like her mom," I replied with a smirk. "We need to focus, babe. It's Saturday. It's getting late, and I don't know when I'll have a chance to get you the clothes again. So let's make it happen." I said sharply. "We can finish this business when we get back," I said, flashing her a smile.

She looked away, then back at me, "Ok, daddy! So, what's your bright idea, anyway?"

I went to my dresser and pulled out the top drawer. Digging deep into the drawer, I found a pair of sweat-pants and a pair of basketball shorts. "Here is my bright idea. Take a pick. We have the grey sweats or the Lakers basketball shorts. Desperate times call for desperate measures," I said seriously, holding an article of clothing in each hand.

"Are you serious?" She asked with a tired look on her face.

"It's only for today. You'll look cute walking through the mall with your husband's sweatpants," I said with a big, cheesy smile.

She chuckled and replied, "There's only one like you. I'll do it, but this time only. And when we get back, you owe me," she said, playfully snatching the sweatpants from me. I wasn't completely sure they could fit her now. That's how much she had grown in a week!

QUESTIONS AND ANSWERS: WHAT FATHERS NEED TO KNOW

Questions:

1. Is it safe to have sex?
2. What do I do if people aren't happy when we announce our pregnancy?
3. My partner wants to do an elaborate event to announce our event, but I don't want to. What should I do?

Answers:

1. Sex is perfectly normal and advised unless told otherwise by a health practitioner. The penetration won't go past the vagina and the baby will be unbothered.

2. Take note of the people you are dealing with. Are they even happy with your relationship? Remain secure in your decision and move on from any negative responses. Inform others of what you expect their response to be at this time—one of love and support.

3. Weigh the pros and cons of disclosing your privacy in an elaborate way with your partner. You need to do what will ultimately bring you peace of mind.

5

NUTS OR NO NUTS? - GENDER REVEAL TIME—THE FIFTH MONTH

WEEK SEVENTEEN

Your Baby

Isn't it funny how quickly 5 months can pass by? It's now week 17 and you're one step closer to winning that bet with your brother that you're having a boy! That's right! This is the month when you'll be finding out the gender of your little one. At sixteen weeks, your baby is the size of an avocado. One week later, we're looking at the size of a pomegranate, which is just a little over 5 inches and weighs in at 5.9 ounces. The baby is growing bigger by the day and is also picking up new tricks along the way. As most of the other organs continue forming to maturity, an increased amount of fat is also being formed around the fetus, which is causing the growth spurts to be exponential. But there's much more going on with your baby than meets the eye. Let's find out some more.

- **Practicing Eating:** Using the fluid inside the amniotic sac, your future great debater is practicing how to suck and swallow when he is idle. Instinctually, baby is sucking their finger in preparation to latch onto their mama's nipple when they leave the womb. He is also practicing swallowing as this is a function he will be using when feeding on the breast or drinking formula from a bottle. Consider this time in the womb as training, where your baby is practicing tirelessly to perfect these skills for when he departs in 4 months.
- **Fingerprints Are Being Perfected:** God forbid your baby has an identity crisis later in life, but at least they will be born with their own unique set of fingerprints. As no two people are the same, a fact proven by the individuality of each person's fingerprints, your special someone will also fall into that category. Within the next week, the padding on the fingertips and toes of your baby will be complete with an individual pattern of swirls and lines. During week 16, we confirmed that the heart of your active fetus

was pumping 25 quarts of blood throughout their body. That sounds like a lot for a vessel the size of an avocado! During this week, the baby's heart is being regulated by their brain, causing the heartbeat to be more regular and less sporadic. Still, their heartbeat is pumping at 140 to 150 beats per minute, which is much faster than the average adult.

Symptoms to Expect at 17 Weeks

You and your partner should take this time to decide when and where you will be going for your next ultrasound to find out the sex of the baby, as this is the time and the season. In a 40-week full-term pregnancy, she is almost halfway there, which means both of you should start sourcing out what kind of childbirth classes you will be attending. You may both be experiencing a bit of anxiety the closer you get to the due date, but that's expected. Keep calm and guide your wife in the best way forward. Try your best to attend the childbirth classes, as you will be needing all the help and advice you can in caring for the infant.

- **Experiencing Weird Dreams:** They say your dreams are a direct result of the thing you think about most. So, undoubtedly, with her little one on the way, your partner isn't thinking about you as often as you might like. Sorry to break it to you. She may be experiencing weird dreams right now, which are largely due to a mixture of her hormones, anticipation, and nerves. As a forewarning, don't be alarmed if she wakes up in the middle of the night with descriptions of otherworldly dreams.

- **Mom's Snoring:** Was that a Harley Davidson? No. That would be your spouse snoring away while captivated by one of those weird dreams again. You're probably confused because she hasn't snored like this since the old days after tequila shots. It's caused by her extreme nasal congestion, which is caused by her hormones. As was suggested earlier, try putting a humidifier in the room or offer her a nasal strip to open her nasal passage so that your night's sleep can return to normal. If all else fails, sleep on the couch! It won't last for long anyway.

WEEK EIGHTEEN

Your Baby

- **Size Upgrade:** There's another leap for your baby at eighteen weeks old! They now weigh close to eight ounces and are 8 1/3 inches tall, roughly the size of a bell pepper. This is an exciting time for you and mom as the baby's genitals are now formed and in place. By the next ultrasound, which should be in the coming weeks, you'll get to see and clearly recognize your baby's ears, nose, eyelids, eyebrows, lips, and hair in place too!

Symptoms to Expect at 18 Weeks

- **Mom's Dizzy Spells:** The immense pressure your partner's body may be under right now can be causing all sorts of physical changes, both externally and internally. One place those changes will take place is in her cardiovascular and nervous systems, where an increased amount of blood is being pumped through her body and to the fetus. Therefore, she may have bouts of dizziness and faintish feelings, especially if she springs up too quickly or overworks herself during exercise. If she suffers from anemia, be sure that she has a balanced work/rest routine.
- **Dealing With Low Blood Pressure:** Low blood pressure can also be the cause of dizziness during mid-pregnancy. As this is a part of the

pregnancy and can't be avoided, some things you can do to assist her will be:

1. Keep her from standing and walking for long periods.
2. Encourage slow and easy movements, especially when she is getting up or laying down.
3. Give her plenty of fluids.
4. Encourage her to keep the water at a lukewarm temperature during baths.

WEEK NINETEEN

Your Baby

If you haven't scheduled your mid-pregnancy ultrasound yet, you have until week 22 to get it done. You are still in the fifth month of pregnancy, and your baby has made it to six inches in length and is over half a pound in weight. For a better perspective, consider the size of a fiber-filled mango—that's how big your baby is now! As you already know, the limbs, organs, and facial features of the fetus are being perfected every day until it's time for the crowning. So, what else can you expect to see between you and your partner about your sweet little mango? Let's find out!

- **Development of the Vernix Caseosa:**
Remember we mentioned the lanugo as the
soft, fine layer of hair that covers the body of
the fetus while in the womb and can sometimes
be present at birth? Well, the lanugo is attached
to a greasy, white protective substance called
the vernix caseosa, which is made up of the hair
from the lanugo. The vernix may sound
disgusting, but its purpose is to protect the
fetus's skin from the surrounding amniotic
fluid, which, without its protection, will leave
your baby looking like a prune at birth—
wrinkled and over-soaked. This usually sheds
as the delivery date approaches.

Symptoms to Expect at Week 19

- **Leg Cramps:** As your spouse gets heavier—as
well as the cozied-up fetus in her womb—the
excess weight can take some getting used to.
She will be experiencing spasms through her
thighs and down to her calves, especially at
night. These stabbing pains hit mostly during
the second and third trimesters. It can be
caused by the fatigue of your partner's leg
muscles from having to carry around all that
extra weight her body isn't used to. Some

simple remedies can be to extend her legs straight out and gently flex her ankles and toes back toward her knees. If you want to be hands-on, you can offer her a soothing leg and calf massage, free of charge!

- **Baby's Kicking Up a Storm:** There's a soccer match championship going on, and it's not on TV! Your little footballer is practicing kicks in mom's tummy, and she can feel each one. She's probably called you over to get in on the action! These movements usually begin between 18 and 22 weeks, and it's a guarantee that as the baby gets bigger, those kicks will be unmistakable.

- **Hip Pain:** In addition to leg cramps and tummy kicks, mom is possibly going through intense hip pain now. This is due to the release of hormones that relax the ligaments in and around the hip area. The best and simplest method for relief from this will be to sleep on her side with a few pillows between her knees. This should offer some much-needed relief.

WEEK TWENTY

Your Baby

You two finally made it to the halfway mark of 20 weeks! Though your partner is still in the fifth month, doctors count your pregnancy by weeks, with 40 weeks being full term. Therefore, you only have 20 more weeks to go. Moms should always leave room for the possibility of giving birth two weeks before or two weeks after the projected due date. You just never know how comfortable your little one is inside that thing.

- **Baby's Size Increase:** Growing steadily at a rapid pace, your once peanut-sized baby is now half the length of a 12-inch ruler, roughly around 6.5 inches. He's also inching closer to a whole pound, weighing in at a little over 11 ounces. Picture a fully matured banana or a sweet potato to get a better idea of the length. It's a good thing bananas don't make mom hurl anymore!
- **Anatomy Scan (Moment of Truth):** Now, for the moment you, your spouse, and everyone else who knows you're expecting has been waiting for—the gender reveal! The second-trimester ultrasound is also known as the anatomy scan, and it will confirm to you the sex

of your fetus—whether it is a boy or a girl. The anatomy scan is usually done during the second trimester between weeks 18 and 22. The focus is primarily on the gender of the child for most parents, but the fetus's other major organs are also being scanned and measured to ensure there are no abnormalities. Going back to the external genitals of the baby, this is the week where your little girl (if that's the gender) will have eggs in her tiny ovaries; and if it's a boy, their testicles will drop soon.

Symptoms to Expect at Week 20

- **Mom's Raging Appetite:** Now that nausea and food aversions are a thing of the past, your partner will be making up for lost time with an increased appetite. If you notice a sudden change in her food choices in the second trimester, encourage it. She needs to regain her strength as well as nourish the baby. Along with all the bacon, eggs, and steak, she will be eating, be sure to incorporate a healthy dose of vitamin C into her diet.
- **Mom's Itchy Skin:** Has your partner been scratching a lot more in recent times? I can assure you that it's not your fault for not doing

the laundry properly! During the mid to late parts of the pregnancy, your partner's skin stretches around her belly and breast area as the baby grows larger and requires more space. This also results in stretch marks in the exact same areas. Be warned, though—scratching will only make the sensation worse. A few tips for relief include applying an ice pack or a cool, wet towel, using aloe vera cream or fragrance-free lotions, and seeking advice from your healthcare practitioner about any anti-itch medications that are safe during pregnancy.

THE GREAT "REVEALING" ULTRASOUND

For some couples, this is one of the most pivotal parts of the pregnancy: the gender reveal. The genitalia of the fetus have been forming since week 11 and now, at week 20, are fully formed. Now it is time to see if mom will be getting a girl to doll up or if dad will be getting a boy as most fathers want. However, it's important to note that regardless of the baby's gender, they should be loved and accepted for the mere fact of being healthy.

Commonly referred to as the anatomy scan, this is done between 18 and 22 weeks and its purpose is to capture images and take measurements of the baby's growing organs and limbs. Some of the main ones include the:

- face
- brain
- spine
- heart
- kidney
- chest
- stomach
- bladder
- genitals
- hands
- feet

The process takes up to 45 minutes, or sometimes more than an hour, to complete and is done by a sonographer rubbing gel onto your partner's belly and applying a transducer onto the gelled area to get the ultrasound images.

Although the focal point for many couples is the baby's gender, an anatomy scan's main function is to check for critical abnormalities, such as heart defects, spinal defects, Down syndrome, or other genetic disorders. Also, depending on the positioning of the baby during the ultrasound scan, the images may still be unclear to prove what the baby's gender is. So, for some couples, you'll have to exercise a little extra patience! But for most future parents curious to know, the ultrasound technician can pinpoint whether the images reveal a labia and clitoris or a penis and testicles, with the correct positioning and cooperation of your baby.

Ensure that you and your partner have agreed to know the sex of the baby beforehand. Not everyone is the same, and some people prefer to know the baby's gender after birth. Discuss your wishes as well as your partner's to be on the same page.

DOCUMENTING THE JOURNEY

During this memorable and fascinating journey of child growth during pregnancy, you can make it even more exciting by documenting each phase. During these 40 weeks (9 to 10 months), there is so much awesomeness taking place that you can show your baby when they're older or use to remind your spouse of the times you shared. You can do so by making a video documentary or by taking photos to track her progress. Also, decide together on whether you're doing a daily, weekly, or monthly documentary. You can even vlog the entire journey and post it on your social media (if that's her thing). If she wants to keep it private until it's absolutely impossible, that's also perfectly fine!

A great way is to do before-and-after photos or videos and mark significant milestones, like the first, second, and third trimesters. Comparison photos of her stomach growth are great ways of capturing how much progress has taken place. Your partner can add in her own flair and personality while using a chalkboard, whiteboard, or letterboard to communicate the period of pregnancy.

This is meant to be a fun exercise the two of you can collaborate on together—great for bonding as a family! Even if you're welcoming your first baby, trust that they will be there every step of the journey with you.

MOM IS CATCHING THE SNIFFLES MUCH MORE

By now, it's no secret that pregnancy is the cause of a massive change in your partner's body. It's being temporarily reconstructed to house and cultivate a whole new life. These changes affect many areas of your spouse, including her immune system. This can lead to her being infected with influenza quite often, although those changes are for the protection of the baby. As a matter of fact, when mom gets a cold, the baby has superb reinforcements as protection—mom's immune system, their own immune system, and the placenta.

- **Common Flu Symptoms:** Flu symptoms for your partner during pregnancy are the same as for an average person. They include a high fever, a dry cough, a sore throat, nasal congestion, headaches, body aches, and fatigue.

- **Flu Treatments:** According to the Centers for Disease Control (CDC), the best preventative measure for the flu is the influenza vaccine shot. The CDC urges pregnant women to get the vaccine to protect themselves and their babies. Over the counter (OTC) drugs can be helpful, but mothers are urged to consult with a health practitioner before using them. Expecting mothers should stay clear of pharmaceuticals like Aspirin, ibuprofen, and Aleve, and decongestants like pseudoephedrine and phenylephrine. Safe alternatives include OTC saline nasal sprays, honey, natural throat lozenges, menthol rubs, and humidifiers.

- **Preventative Measures:** You can do your part, dad, by helping to prevent the flu before it even springs up. As you're aware, a balanced diet is super important for your partner, so things like fruits and vegetables rich in vitamin C, lots of clear fluids, and sufficient rest are all key for flu prevention. Taking her prenatal vitamins and getting at least 20 minutes of exercise a day are also effective preventative measures.

READY FOR A BABYMOON?

For those who are hearing this term for the first time, a babymoon is essentially the same as a honeymoon, except you're not taking a romantic getaway with your lover after marriage; it's more of a vacation with your baby before delivery. Of course, this doesn't mean that your spouse will be embarking on a trip with just her and the baby. It's a family affair that is meant to be a bonding experience to remind you of how far you've come as a couple and a family. The idea of babymoons has become popular among the Hollywood elite and has gained popularity since then.

- **Timing:** Before deciding upon a babymoon with your partner, you first want the timing to be right. According to the American College of Obstetricians and Gynecologists, the best time to plan your excursion is between 14 and 20 weeks, or typically in the second trimester. This is to avoid the nagging symptoms of morning sickness, fatigue, and food aversions that accompany the first trimester.
- **Final Destination:** Once you have consulted her healthcare provider about your plans to travel and she has no reservations about your partner's current state, you can begin choosing

the right destination. You can choose to go overseas, a tropical beach hideaway, a historic site, an Airbnb rental, or an exotic restaurant. It's wise not to choose something too far away or with complicated layovers that will be exhausting for your already fatigued partner. A cruise is also a perfect getaway that will only last a few days but will be an unforgettable experience. You want to be sure that there are professional medical personnel on board should the need arise, as well as at the ports you will be visiting. It's also wise to inform her doctor of your plans to travel. Especially since the COVID-19 pandemic, her doctor will be the best person to let you know if a vaccine can or should be taken by your partner, as certain vaccines are required for various forms of travel.

QUESTIONS AND ANSWERS: WHAT FATHERS NEED TO KNOW

Questions:

1. Is it normal to lose interest in sex while my partner is pregnant?

2. I'm afraid of hurting her or the baby during sex; what can I do?

3. What if we disagree about finding out our baby's gender?

4. What if I'm disappointed with the gender of my baby? Will that change? Am I horrible?

Answers:

1. Having sex won't hurt the baby. It's actually advised for partners to have sex as it has been proven to lubricate your partner and cause an easy delivery.

2. Engage in respectful communication and express your feelings on the matter.

3. Evaluate your feelings and allow yourself to work through them. It's normal to be disappointed in the gender of your baby, especially if you had dreams of raising a certain one.

6

I FELT THE KICK!—THE SIXTH MONTH

"Everything grows rounder and wider and weirder, and I sit here in the middle of it all and wonder who in the world you will turn out to be."

— CARRIE FISHER

WEEK TWENTY-ONE

Your Baby

You are now over the hump and heading towards the light at the end of the tunnel, except this tunnel signals the birth of your baby. I wouldn't say things are expected to get easier from here on out, but the worst is over to an extent. At 21 weeks, your baby is still growing with tremendous speed—coming in at a weight of 14 ounces and a height of close to 11 inches! For a visual comparison, baby is the size of a large banana or carrot, and that growth isn't in vain. It comes with its perks. Let's get more into the specifications.

- **Developing Tastebuds:** Your baby senses that they have reached another chapter of development with the formation of their taste buds. With that, baby is already practicing for the first taste of breastmilk by swallowing amniotic fluid, a practice that not only aids in swallowing and digestion but also provides nutrition and hydration. Researchers have found that at this time, your baby is able to taste everything being ingested by your partner, whether that be something savory, spicy, or sweet. They also found that your baby will be eager to eat food with the same tastes they have been experiencing in the womb.

- **Hand-Eye Coordination:** Right now, your baby is more alive than ever, and if you haven't already, you'll be feeling their activity with fluttering movements becoming stronger and more intentional as time goes by. Go, karate kid! Soon enough, dad, you'll be able to feel

those kicks and punches more often. Possibly
every time your baby gets accustomed to you
and hears your voice. This coordination is due
to the neurons that are now connected between
the brain and muscles, giving your future
gymnast greater control over limb movements.

- **Eyebrows Forming:** Your baby's eyebrows may
  be forming in their fullness and growing in just
  like their hair. However, baby's eyelids are still
  closed while the pigmentation in her eyelids is
  being produced.

Symptoms to Expect at Week 21

- **Bold, Beautiful Stretch Marks:** As promised,
  the expansion of your partner's abdomen and
  enlargement of her breasts are causing stretch
  marks, which have also been the cause of her
  compulsive itching. If you've been observing
  her body, you'll see that they have also shown
  up on her stomach, butt, thighs, and hips. Not
  every woman gets stretch marks, though, and
  their appearance has a lot to do with the
  complexion of the person. They range in colors
  from pink, red, and purple to reddish-brown or
  brown streaks. However, they can be more
  pronounced if the mother gains weight rapidly,

which is why it's best to add on the calories incrementally after the first trimester. Mom can apply cocoa butter to the stretch marks, although there's not a proven method of stopping them. Despite the negative feedback that stretch marks make your spouse undesirable, a real man should see it as a badge of honor for her to celebrate. Stretch marks should be a symbol of beauty and strength and a reminder of the special quality a woman is given—the ability to birth life.

- **Exercise Is Key:** It can't be stressed enough how important exercise is during pregnancy. Especially now that your partner's appetite has returned and her fatigue is gone, she should be keeping her blood circulation going by walking for at least 30 minutes a day. And you can definitely encourage that. Constipation is likely to surface every now and then, and physical activity like a brisk walk every day is sure to ease her bowels. In addition, it gets the baby's blood pumping too. Who doesn't want an adventure?

- **Nutritious Meals, Please:** While it has been suggested that your wife should gain weight during the pregnancy, it's not a license to start chugging back all the wrong foods. Yes, she is

supposed to be gaining weight by default
because of the baby, but maintaining a healthy
diet while slowly gaining weight is still a
priority. This can look like substituting certain
foods for others, such as baked yams or
plantains for potato chips and fries, a frozen
yogurt smoothie for ice cream, or boiled fish
for fried chicken. Don't forget to add a packed
fruit bowl!

WEEK TWENTY-TWO

Your Baby

- **Baby's Size Increase:** In just one week, your
  miracle baby has gained weight and now
  weighs more than a pound. In terms of height,
  baby is nearing the full-length grade school
  ruler at around 11.5 inches and is looking more
  like a red bell pepper. Besides the sizeable
  increase, there is much more progress taking
  place, such as your baby's grip, vision, and
  hearing all strengthening simultaneously. They
  might be grabbing hold of the umbilical cord to
  strengthen their grip and may be highly
  sensitive to light—although inside the womb it
  is mostly dark. Additionally, dad should also be

feeling those kicks a lot more, which you are probably eager to continue feeling!

Symptoms to Expect at Week 22

- **Mom's Foot Growth:** Whichever one of you realizes it first, it'll become clear that your partner's feet have grown (but not to Sasquatch size). If she is still able to see her feet over her swelling belly, she'll discover that not only are her feet swollen, but they have maybe grown a few inches and could possibly remain that way. Her hormones are again the cause of this phenomenon, the hormone relaxin in particular. Relaxin is the pregnancy hormone responsible for loosening the ligaments and joints around the pelvic area to allow the baby's smooth passage. Relaxin shares its love all the way down to the ligaments in your spouse's feet, loosening them, which results in a larger shoe size. When shopping for her, she should keep in mind that a comfortable pair of ballet flats or sandals that are comfortable and spacious are better for keeping her balance, as this hormone is also known to make mom a bit clumsy. As swelling can be an accompanying symptom, encourage her to keep both feet elevated so the fluid doesn't accumulate in one area.

- **An Acne Outbreak:** Acne is also a common symptom for expecting mothers between the first and second trimester. Once again, hormones, androgens this time, are to blame for the outbreak. Androgens cause the glands in the skin to produce an oily substance called sebum, which is liable to clog pores and cause breakouts.

- **Warding off the Tummy touchers:** Once you've felt your baby's kicks, not even you can keep your hands off your wife's baby bump. But just as her womb is for your baby only, her belly and body should be for your hands only. Therefore, regardless of whether friends, family, co-workers, or whoever else wants to touch her tummy, even if she doesn't mind, you should set boundaries. Most women are sensitive about people touching their tummies (maternal instinct). If your spouse is one of those women, especially if she is shy, support her by telling people assertively to not do it. You just never know the intentions of some people.

WEEK TWENTY-THREE

Your Baby

- **Baby's Size Increase:** If you're looking for a miraculous fruit to make juice for your spouse, try grapefruit or a large mango. Not only are they rich in vitamin C, but they're also the size of your baby at twenty-three weeks. That's right! The baby's growth spurt has increased yet again, and baby now weighs 1 ¼ pounds at a height of over 12 inches. It seems we've found the future star player for the WNBA team!

- **Taking In the Sounds:** One of the reasons why "dada" is normally the first word out of a baby's mouth is that when they start to hear the outside world, the first sounds baby hears are low-toned base voices, like that of a male or a barking dog (ignore the comparison). Your baby, boy or girl, can hear low-pitch voices clearer than female voices. So, if you keep telling her, "dada," your voice is likely to stay stuck in her mind.

Symptoms to Expect at Week 23

- **Skin Discoloration:** Along with a new trimester comes new pregnancy symptoms caused by the same pregnancy hormones. It's skin discoloration but not the same as stretch marks. This skin discoloration is called "dark line" or *linea nigra*, and it appears more commonly in darker-toned women. It runs along their belly, from the belly button to the pubic area. This is the same hormone that causes the darkening of her nipples and may even cause discoloration on her face. The discoloration usually fades a few months after delivery.

- **Hazy Pregnancy Brain:** Has your spouse been misplacing things like her purse, your keys, or maybe even hospital documents? Maybe the once scheduled and efficient home-keeper isn't able to multitask like before. Well, that's because of what's known as "mom brain" or "pregnancy brain," and, yes, it's caused by her hormones. The chronic fatigue and constant urination preventing her from getting a good night's sleep can also be the reason for the brain fog. Excitement about the pregnancy can also be the reason for her lack of focus. If you're more of a tech-geek, assist her by putting reminders on her phone calendar, encouraging her to write things down, helping to organize her day, and feeding her lots of ginkgo biloba and omega-3-rich foods. And if you're a jokester like me, encourage her to laugh it off. Having a sense of humor will put her at ease and take her mind off the fact that she may be a bit forgetful now.

- **Rest and Relaxation:** It's understandable that your partner will be filled with a bit of anxiety over the life of her young one growing in her womb. But having her nerves go haywire isn't beneficial to her mental health or the baby's environment. If you were honest with yourself, you'd admit that you too are feeling the pre-delivery angst. Do yourself a favor by remaining centered and leading your partner to do the same. Suggest that she use coping mechanisms like deep breathing exercises or simply sitting quietly for a few minutes, imagining herself in a serene setting. Slowing down her day and doing deep breathing are great ways to de-stress as well. You can also accompany her to keep your mind settled.

WEEK TWENTY-FOUR

Your Baby

- **Growing Big and Strong:** Ever closer to the big day, your baby is growing in leaps and bounds. What was once the size of a blueberry has grown into a full ear of corn measuring 12.68 inches from crown-to-rump and weighing close to 1.5 pounds. Your tiny peanut is getting ready to add on more size, muscle, and baby fat. With their limbs and facial features reaching perfection, all that's missing now is to plump up.
- **Facial Features Being Refined:** Although still small in size, the baby's face is being formed to perfection! It's safe to say that if you saw your baby right now, both you and your partner will know whose genes were stronger by their facial features. It's equipped with eyelashes, eyebrows, and hair.

Symptoms to Expect at 24 Weeks

- **Carpal Tunnel Syndrome:** Have you ever slept on your hands and woken up with that numb, tingly, pin-prickly feeling coursing through your wrists and fingers? If yes, it is possibly carpal tunnel syndrome. While it's normally associated with specific tasks that demand repetitive movement, such as typing, it arises in pregnant women through accumulated fluids that are dispersed throughout the body when lying down. As a result, she may experience symptoms associated with carpal tunnel syndrome. To find relief, encourage her to prop her hands on a pillow instead of sleeping on them. Also encourage her to avoid typing and other activities requiring repetitive hand motions.

- **Itchy Palms:** Pregnancy comes with a lot of strange physical adaptations that make you wonder what some of them have to do with pregnancy to begin with. The red, itchy skin many women experience will leave you wondering what caused it. But if you've been reading through, you will have already guessed the culprit is hormones. The itchy redness can be bunched into the same bracket as the metallic taste in her mouth, increased saliva, and bigger feet. The sad thing is that there's no known cure for it except delivery—once the baby is out, the itching stops! Until then, dissuade her from taking lingering, hot showers or being overheated as it only makes the itching worse. If it's really bothering her, she can apply an ice pack for a few minutes throughout the day.

- **Preparing the Nursery:** With roughly only 16 weeks remaining, mom might have a maternal unction to begin preparing the baby's nursery. That means your brawn will be required for mounting the crib, organizing, cleaning, and making babyproofing paces all throughout your home. In whatever you do, ensure the safety of the baby comes first.

PREPARING FOR THE GLUCOSE TEST

As the time draws nearer to the birth, a major test that will need to be conducted for the safety of both mom and the baby is the glucose test. You may be wondering what it's all about. This test screens for gestational diabetes (GD) which, according to the CDC, affects up to 10 percent of women in pregnancies.

It's basically a test done to determine if a pregnant woman's blood glucose level is above average. Glucose is another word for sugar, and if the sugar in her blood is too high, she may be at risk for developing gestational diabetes (GD). The prevention of GD is one of the reasons why it's necessary to maintain a healthy balance of diet and exercise with your partner during pregnancy, as these are two of the main methods of controlling her blood sugar.

So, if your wife is known for having a sweet tooth, you will need to be even keener in watching her sugar intake. It's a serious diagnosis with severe repercussions for both mom and baby, such as macrosomia (which increases the chance of a C-section), jaundice, stillbirth, and a higher risk of your child developing type 2 diabetes later in life.

In preparation for the test, your partner will be required to stay without eating or drinking anything besides water for 8 to 14 hours prior to the test. She will then be asked to consume 100 grams of a liquid that contains glucose, which likely doesn't have the most pleasant taste. Then, the doctor will draw her blood once before drinking the glucose and three times thereafter. If your partner is a coward when it comes to needles, be her rock of support, as there will be a lot of pin-pricking.

ORGANIZING THE BABY REGISTRY

In case you haven't already, you want to get moving on preparing a baby registry. Basically, it's a list of items that parents-to-be create for friends and family to choose gifts from. You will want to keep your partner close by with this one as her "mom instincts" may have already kicked in and she will know exactly what is needed. The experience may be fun, however, most people pre-package their registries online through stores like Bed, Bath, and Beyond; Amazon; Costco; and Crate and Barrel.

However, if you and your spouse do decide to prepare your own from scratch, there are quite a few things you will want to consider, such as the quantity of items, needs vs. wants, and your lifestyle and budget and remember to focus on the first six months post-delivery. The most important things to have on the list include a stroller, baby carrier, car seat, diapers, wipes, first-aid kits, crib sheets, toys, pajamas, and onesies. Aim to keep things as simple as possible and ensure that you cover the essentials first. Everything else after that is optional.

SIGNS OF PRETERM LABOR

The average length of a full-term pregnancy is 40 weeks, give or take. Most doctors give an allowance of a couple of weeks before or after the expected due date. However, babies born before 37 weeks tend to be more susceptible to problems breathing, eating, and maintaining a decent body temperature. That's why it's better for your baby to stay in the womb a few weeks past the due date than to be born three weeks before, because preterm labor can result in premature birth. Premature labor is triggered between the 20th and 37th weeks when the mouth of the uterus (womb) is opened earlier than normal by uterine contractions caused by the cervix.

Before getting into the telltale signs of premature labor, here are a few factors that may increase your spouse's chances of having a premature birth:

- smoking
- being a teen or being over 40 years old
- being extremely overweight or underweight before pregnancy
- alcohol or drug usage during pregnancy
- family history of premature labor
- pre-existing health conditions like diabetes, high blood pressure, preeclampsia, or other infections

Now that you know some of the reasons behind the causes of premature labor, let's delve into a few of the warning signs that indicate that your partner may be at risk of premature labor:

- consecutive contractions that happen frequently, every 10 minutes or more
- a low, dull backache
- menstrual cramps that may come with or without diarrhea
- vaginal spotting or light bleeding
- pelvic or abdominal pressure
- increased vaginal discharge of a watery, mucous, bloody mixture

If any of these symptoms display themselves in your partner more than three weeks before the due date, contact a healthcare provider immediately. Even if it's a false alarm, it's still better to be safe than sorry.

☆ DON'T DRINK THE KOOL-AID: A PERSONAL STORY

We were back in Dr. Longh's office now at twenty-four weeks into the pregnancy. My little Rocky had been making movements in my wife's belly, and I felt like the happiest man alive! But my dreams of a future world champion boxer were cut short after the anatomy scan a few weeks ago revealed that we're having a girl. Don't get me wrong—I'll love my daughter to pieces—but I had plans for me and my boy, you know? Was I wrong for thinking this way? I feel like she's not even out of the womb yet, and I'm already projecting thoughts of rejection onto her. Regardless of the sex, I just want our baby to be healthy and strong.

Dr. Longh's secretary finally called us into his office. "Hi, there! My favorite pregnant couple. Come, take a seat, both of you," he motioned to the navy-blue vintage chairs facing his desk. He continued, "Well, as you know, today is the glucose test for the beautiful lady," he said, smiling warmly at my wife, who smiled courteously in return of the compliment. He then shifted his gaze to me, "And you, Papi Chulo... did you ensure that your wife refrained from food and drink for the period of time required?" He inquired.

"Yes, of course. It took some convincing, but Papi got Mami to listen," I replied, as I glanced over at my wife. She was glowing right now in a way I had never seen before. It made me want to love her even more—big belly, stretch marks and all.

"That's very good to hear. So, let's proceed. As you know, there is a three-step process to this glucose test. Once again, we are checking to see if her glucose levels are at a decent level. If it is too high, this puts her at risk for gestational diabetes and even C-sections. Nobody wants this, right?"

His rhetorical question was met with an anxious look from my wife, to which I nodded to quietly offer encouragement. "No doc, we do NOT," I emphasized. I wanted this to be as natural and uncomplicated as possible.

"Perfecto! Let's begin." He left briefly and went to the patient's room to return with a bright orange glass of liquid that looked like a highly concentrated packet of orange Tang juice mix. "Here you go," he said as he served the drink to my wife. "Drink this, my dear, and we'll move on to the blood sampling." he directed.

"Ok, Dr. Longh," my wife replied cheerfully. "I hope this thing tastes as good as it looks," she said as she reluctantly put the glass to her mouth.

I glanced at my watch briefly to see how our time was going because I had lunch reservations booked for us afterward. Then suddenly, the unthinkable happened. "Bllaahh...Gggrraahh!" My wife vomited all over Dr. Longh's desk.

"Babe, what's wrong? You just threw up your breakfast," I said as I reached to take the glass from her and rub her back.

"Oh my gosh, Dr. Longh. I'm so sorry. I don't know what happened. This thing tastes horrible!" She cried.

Dr. Longh seemed unphased, as if he had seen this happen many times before. "That's ok, that's ok. I'll get it cleaned up. Maybe I'll give you a different flavor. We'll hope that helps."

That day, it took three different flavors and three regurgitations before my wife was finally able to stomach the glucose juice. By the time she finished the blood work, she was noticeably exhausted and hungry. I had to change our dining reservation to go, and we went home to eat. Let's just say she didn't look at an orange drink the same, even months after giving birth!

QUESTIONS AND ANSWERS: WHAT FATHERS NEED TO KNOW

Questions:

1. Are there ways to prevent preterm labor?
2. What happens if my baby is born early?
3. Can the baby see my penis?

Answers:

1. There are no known ways to prevent preterm labor, but certain actions can help, like not smoking, reducing the stress of your partner, and encouraging your partner to brush and

floss her teeth daily, as gum disease is linked to preterm delivery.

2. Premature babies can catch up to their peers, but they do have a higher risk of health problems.

3. No. Your baby has no idea of the intimate moments between you and your partner besides the rocking motion, which baby probably enjoys.

7

PEDIATRICIAN? THE BABY ISN'T EVEN HERE YET!—THE SEVENTH MONTH

WEEK TWENTY-FIVE

"In the pregnancy process, I have come to realize how much of the burden is on the female partner. She's got a construction zone going on in her belly."

— AL ROKER

Truer words were never spoken—even men get traumatized at the thought of dealing with the magnitude of symptoms a woman goes through. Then, at the end of it all, she experiences the ultimate conflict of pleasure and pain all in one go. It's almost lights, camera, and action for your baby, the star of the show.

Your Baby

- **Growing in Leaps and Bounds:** At 25 weeks pregnant, your partner is 6 months pregnant, which means there are only 3 months (or 15 weeks) left to go. Guess who's graduated to the size of an eggplant! You guessed it, your baby is now about 13 inches long and more than 1.5 pounds in weight. Even better, baby is going to start looking the part with the extra baby fat latching onto them right now.

- **Lungs and Reflexes at Work:** The more baby grows, the more they continue to be an awesome wonder. Daddy's little angel is now developing startle reflexes to go along with those sweet facial features that are in their final stages, including heads of hair thickening out. While still practicing the sucking and swallowing technique with the amniotic fluid, baby's lungs are being developed with more blood vessels, preparing them to one day soon take their first breath of fresh air. Though they aren't yet fully developed, efforts in the womb will be rewarded.

- **Use the Nose Daddy Gave You:** Your baby's nose is also at work as the lungs and nostrils begin working in sync, enabling baby to take practice breaths. While it may be hard to practice breathing in fluid (unless you're a fish), this is the only form of "breathing" they have, so it'll have to do for now.
- **Getting Chubby:** Surely, your partner won't make it through 40 weeks of gruesome symptoms and turmoil to have a baby come out looking like a Benjamin Button prototype. That's not what either of you had in mind. That's why your darling baby will be trading in their long, slender build and wrinkled skin for a fattened physique and soft skin. So, don't worry, baby will be coming out looking like an actual newborn.

Symptoms to Expect at Week 25

- **Hemorrhoids:** This may be one of the most uncomfortable symptoms one can experience during pregnancy, although that's up for debate! Hemorrhoids are a form of varicose veins, found in the rectum, that almost all pregnant women have to endure and are brought about by the enlarged uterus pressing against that area. While they are not life-threatening, they can result in rectal bleeding and can be itchy and painful. The best way to prevent this thorn in the flesh is to provide lots of fiber-rich food for your wife, such as fruits, vegetables, and whole grains. Also, she should be flushing her system with lots of fluid to keep a regular stool, as hemorrhoids are also caused by constipation (another pregnancy symptom). She can also do Kegel pelvic exercises, which can help as well.

WEEK TWENTY-SIX

Your Baby

- **Getting Bigger and Losing Space:** Now the size of an acorn squash, 26 weeks has never looked better on a baby. Your little one now weighs in at a whopping 2 pounds and measures over 14 inches in length. All this growth will have baby feeling a bit limited in terms of space in your wife's uterus, but they're still not done growing yet.
- **Eyes Can See Clearly Now:** At long last, your baby's eyes are finally beginning to open. They've been under construction behind sealed

eyelids, especially for the formation of the retina, without which they wouldn't be able to clearly see an image. So, at this point, your baby's eyes are fully functional and can see all that's happening in its surroundings. The only problem is that there's not much to see in the uterus. For the curious dad, try taking a flashlight and shining it on your spouse's belly. You might get a kick out of it—literally!

- **Mom's Outstanding Belly Button:** Mom's belly button may be about ready to pop out of her belly. Her once normal inside navel is now protruding outward, which is likely caused by the placement of her uterus, about 2.5 inches above her belly button. Now it makes perfect sense. If your spouse has a navel piercing, it's best to remove it. She can revert to looking sexy again after delivery when the baby is out of harm's way and her navel will have shrunk in size.

- **Not-So Sweet Dreams:** Counting sheep for your partner may seem harder now, since they're running away from her, just like her sleep. With the countless physical abnormalities she is dealing with—heartburn, frequent urination, constipation, dizziness, leg cramps, and hemorrhoids—it's understandable why sleep could be evading her. She should try to tire herself out with daytime exercises, go on a walk for fresh air, or limit the fluids she drinks before bedtime. Then, you can go back to hearing her snore.

WEEK TWENTY-SEVEN: LEAVING THE SECOND TRIMESTER

Your Baby

- **Lager Than... Cauliflower:** Yeah! How does it feel to know that you made it all the way to the fourth quarter with your wife and didn't cave in? Granted, you may have considered calling it quits after the first few weeks of the first trimester when you realized you had knocked up the bride of chucky (figuratively speaking), but you stuck it out and here we are, at week 27! To give you an idea of how much your baby has grown, consider a head of cauliflower— that's about 14.5 inches and almost 2.5 pounds.
- **The Baby Can Hear Clearly:** Despite their hearing being muffled thanks to the thick coating of the vernix, their auditory development is mature enough to differentiate your spouse's voice from your own. Now is a

great time to get a head start on singing nursery rhymes, reading children's stories, or playing soothing music to familiarize them with different sounds. Here's a fun exercise you can try together. Put your ear to your partner's tummy and listen for your baby's heartbeat. If you've already picked out a name, start calling baby by it and wait for a response. Bonding starts right now!

- **Hiccups and Tastebuds:** At 27 weeks, your baby's taste buds are more developed than ever before. Baby may even be responding to the types of foods you consume with a minor spasm. Your spouse can do a trial run by eating something spicy and waiting for their reaction. The fetus will realize the difference in taste through the amniotic fluid.

The baby may also respond to different-tasting foods by hiccupping. But that doesn't mean baby is affected at all. That's their way of saying, "That was different! But nice."

Symptoms to Expect at Week 27

- **Mom's Five O' Clock Shadow:** The title is a bit overdramatized, but the same hormones that caused the acne outbreak, called androgens, are also responsible for the increased rate of growth in facial and body hair. So, if you realize it getting out of hand and her belly is getting too big to see her toes, offer to shave those hard-to-reach places with her. That way, you can both be satisfied!

- **To Soothe a Heat Rash:** Heat rash can also be a direct result of mom's already-heated pregnant physique, clammy skin caused by perspiration, and the rubbing of skin-to-skin or skin-to-fabric. All of the above can cause the red, bumpy, prickly heat rash to flare up. The best soothing methods are to stay cool as much as possible (be glad if your spouse walks around the house naked) by the clothing she wears, use a cool compress, or use calamine lotion, which is known to soothe itchy irritations.

WEEK TWENTY-EIGHT: ENTER THE THIRD TRIMESTER

Enter your final destination: the third trimester. Consider this the last leg of the race for you and especially for your spouse, who has suffered the most. There is still much more growth to be done and preparing for the arrival of the family's newest member, but 7 months is a milestone worth recognizing. Your spouse will most likely have a checkup every two weeks, which will switch to one a week after week 36 and leading up to the delivery. Stay tuned for what's to be expected.

Your Baby

- **Baby Is a Lettuce Head:** Still a work in progress, your baby has graduated in size to that of a head of lettuce. Weighing about 2.25 pounds and 15 inches long, you have an exceptional growth spurt on your hands that will only improve in the coming weeks.
- **Positioned for Release:** Even your baby knows when it's a change in season. Like a transformed butterfly, baby is ready to be released from the cocoon of uterus confinement they've been made grow in. Over the next few weeks, baby will be transitioning

their position from feet-down to head-down, ready to be launched from the emergency exit. It seems baby is just as eager as you and your spouse are to meet each other in person, outside the womb.

- **Dreaming of You Tonight:** No one knows for sure who your baby is dreaming of; they've seen no one on the outside after all. But one thing is for sure, baby's brain has been adding billions of new nerve cells, especially since their eyes have been opened. Your little one is experiencing rapid eye movement in addition to an increase in brain weight, which means something is happening up there.

Symptoms to Expect at Week 28

- **Sciatica Pain Is Real:** There's never been a dull moment in the entire pregnancy. But it's about to get even more eventful, and maybe a little irritating for mom. In addition to all the uncomfortable body ailments she may be enduring, as the baby gets into position, as the uterus continues to grow, it may be resting on her sciatic nerve. Found in the lower part of the spine, the sciatic nerve sends a sharp, shooting pain beginning in the buttocks and trailing down the back of her leg when triggered. This is known as sciatica, and the baby has no idea what's going on.

- **Mom's Skin Sensitivity:** In the same way that those peeving hormones caused your spouse to suddenly be intolerable to the food she once loved, the same effect is occurring with her skin. Pregnancy hormones are now attacking her skin, causing some areas to be dry and flaky, while others are pimple-filled with heat rash. Her sensitivity may react to common things like sunlight, heat, chlorine, and other chemicals, or her favorite body cream could be the culprit. As a remedy, she can apply calamine lotion to the affected areas and avoid products with fragrances, dyes, or additives. That includes perfumes too.

CHOOSING A BABY NAME

It can be a huge sigh of relief to know that you have reached the point of deciding upon baby names. That means you're that much closer to holding that name in the form of your child in your arms. It's so exciting! After learning the sex of your baby during the anatomy scan ultrasound, it makes your decision-making much easier.

Now that you know the gender of your baby, you and your partner can first talk openly about the options that are available. You can begin by jotting down a set of names that you absolutely dread. At least now, you'll both agree on what you don't want to call your child. By eliminating the non-negotiables, you can now focus on the potential candidates.

You and your partner can now think of at least 10 of the best names that come to mind that you've found while doing research and consider them your favorites. Keep in mind that when choosing a baby name, you need to consider the culture of your partner, religious beliefs, traditional family names, and the meaning of the name. Remember that whatever you decide to call your child, you will be calling them the meaning of that name every day for the rest of their life. So, don't pick a name that sounds cool, but literally means "the cursed one" or "troublemaker." You want to pick names that can help positively mold their character and even shape their destiny. Here are a few things to consider when choosing:

1. **Avoid Popular/Trending Names:** Your child is an individual, and you want their name to be unique but not to the point of being grossly misspelled or too farfetched to pronounce. Trending names also lose their appeal after time

because what is hot today may be gone tomorrow. Choose a name with a character that you want to define your little one by.

2. **Classic Names Are Cool**: There are different examples of classic names. When I say classic, I don't mean to name your child John, Peter, or Mary. They're not bad names, but other culturally traditional names, such as Akeem, Malik, Zion, or Rashad for boys and Aaliyah, Naima, Rachel, and Tiani for girls.

3. **Consider Your Culture and Family Tree:** If one of your partner's names has been passed down through generations and they want to keep it, you may have to compromise somewhere. But in the case of culture, if your partner is African American, Caribbean, Asian, or any other culture, they might want to honor that with a name representing it.

4. **Look Up Name Meanings:** If you're spiritual, you may not mind that the name Isaiah means "God is high" or that the name Sue means "graceful lily" or that Leanne means "to twine around." Whatever floats your boat works, but be prepared when people ask you the definition of the name!

If you and your partner are having a hard time agreeing on a name, communicate openly about it. Listening to each other's reasons for rejecting a name is needed to move forward. Remember that the baby gets to have a middle name too. So instead of bickering over one name, each partner should choose one and bring them together. That way, you both win!

MISSING YOUR OLD LIFE?

You often hear it said that once you have a baby, your life is basically over. While that is an overly dramatic statement, it is true to a certain extent. If you're serious about being a parent, there are certain lifestyles and habits you're going to feel the need to separate from. Therefore, it's common to feel a bit nostalgic about the life you led prior to having a child.

Of all your friends, if you are the only one who has a child, they're going to have to understand that your life now requires a different level of responsibility. Does it mean that you must cut off your buddies? No, not at all. You can still have a life outside of being a parent, but if you used to go club hopping and get home at 3 o'clock in the morning, then of course that pattern of behavior can't continue.

Communicating with your partner is the best remedy for these feelings. After all, she may also share similar feelings. But if you are both serious about your parental responsibilities, you will find new ways to have fun as a family. You will become so used to parental life after a while that your care-free, childish mentality will be a thing of the past as you realize there is much more to life than living for yourself. Accept your nostalgia and move on to the new life of family and love that awaits you.

KNOWING THE SIGNS OF PREECLAMPSIA

Once your partner enters the later stages of her pregnancy, one of the terms you will need to become familiar with is preeclampsia. It is a condition that comes about when women have high blood pressure, high levels of protein in their urine, and swelling in their hands, feet, and legs.

At its worst, this condition is said to cause eclampsia, which is detrimental to both mother and child and can even be fatal in some instances. There is no known prevention of preeclampsia and only delivery is known to cause it to go away.

A few symptoms to look out for in case you notice them in your spouse include:

208 | JESSE HAYES

- rapid weight gain due to bodily fluid
- shoulder pain
- belly pain
- dizziness
- severe headaches
- urinating less or not at all
- shortness of breath
- chronic vomiting and nausea
- blurry vision and other changes in vision
- fewer platelets in blood

As to the cause of Preeclampsia, there is no definite cause, but some experts believe it may be caused by a defect in the way the placenta works. Others believe poor nutrition and a high body-mass index may also have a part to play, and others conclude that a lack of blood flow to the uterus is to blame.

FINDING A PEDIATRICIAN

It's nearing the time to find a pediatrician for the birth of your baby, and there are a few things you want to keep in mind, especially since the service of a pediatrician doesn't stop when the baby is born. Doctor visits can continue well into the first year of birth. You and your wife want to be sure that you're looking for someone who will be around for the long haul. They will not only aid in your baby's health and wellness but will also assist you in handling certain early-childhood hiccups since you and your spouse have no prior knowledge of childcare (if this is your first child). Ultimately, the same investment you made in finding a spouse with good qualities that was worth your time should also be made in finding a pediatrician who is capable of caring for your child in the long term.

Here are a few considerations to factor in when hunting for a trusted pediatrician for your newborn:

1. Are they certified?
Pediatricians graduate from medical school with either an MD (Doctor of Medicine) or a DO (doctor of osteopathy), which are both degrees that certify and train doctors to diagnose and treat diseases and other illnesses. In addition to a degree, you also want to be sure that the doctors are board certified.

2. Are they in close proximity?
Finding a pediatrician that is close by, or at least in the same vicinity as your living quarters, is best. If you can walk, take a bus, or ride a train to get there, even better. Especially with a newborn, you never know when you might need to run across town in case of an emergency.

3. What are the operating hours?
Availability is of key importance, especially if neither of you is a stay-at-home parent. If your doctor works from 9 a.m. to 5 p.m. like you, then there is no chance that you'll ever make a successful appointment. So, you'll need to find out if the office has an assistant nurse who takes over in their absence. How far in advance do you have to book appointments? Do they take walk-ins?

4. What kind of insurance do they accept?
If you have already gone ahead and added your child to your insurance policy, you want to know whether they accept your insurance. And besides insurance, is it even affordable out of pocket?

5. Who do your family and friends suggest?
If you're seeking to be referred to a reliable pediatrician, you should reach out to friends and family who already have children. They will usually be the most trusted sources to lead you to a reputable pediatrician, especially if they have remained faithful for years.

6. Are they professional and kind?
Before putting your child in the care of anyone, ensure that you vet them thoroughly for their level of professionalism and demeanor. Are they courteous to the patients as well as their staff?

Do they listen carefully to the concerns of their patients, or are they arrogant and dogmatic? If they seem more concerned with your payment than with your child's health, trust what is being presented to you and find someone else who is more genuine.

☆ DOG-LOVER LIKE DADDY: A PERSONAL STORY

"Is she alive in there?" I asked rhetorically.

"Of course she's alive. Don't say stuff like that," my wife responded in a catty manner. "She was moving just this morning," she followed up.

"Yea, when you woke up and ate some food. Of course, she'd move for food … she was probably hungry!" I said to challenge her. She looked at me with a fit of rage. Those hormones again, I tell you. "Come on, babe. Don't be like that. I'm just trying to get you up and moving. Doctors say your baby will take on your attitude and routines from in the womb. So, if you get up and get moving, you might have a future track star on your hands," I said, trying to persuade her to take a walk.

"Ooooh … I want to exercise, but it sucks by myself. I'd rather do it with you, but you're at work all day. Then when you come back, you're tired and there's no point anymore," she said in a complaining tone.

"Tired? Me? Who said I was tired? If you want motivation, baby, let me put you in gear. Let's go right now," I said, watching her with a game face.

"Now?" She confirmed it with a smile.

"Yea. Right now." I confirmed, still waiting for her to get off the bed, which she began to do. "That's right, baby. Let's all get in shape. When the baby comes out, we'll make it a daily routine!" I said eagerly.

"I hear you," she replied as she got dressed in her athletic maternity wear.

We walked casually because I was honestly tired from work, but I wanted to get her and the baby out of the house for a bit. We walked to the nearby children's park and saw a vacant bench, so we stopped briefly.

"I bet you my lil' girl is kicking around now," I said playfully as I put my hand on her protruding stomach. I felt for any signs of movement … a kick, a slap, something. But she was motionless.

"She's probably sleeping now," my wife suggested. "I observed her routine and she usually naps at this time," she said confidently.

"Ok, ok. Look at you! Mommy taking notes on her daughter," I said calmly. My hand was still on her stomach as we spoke when just then, a grey dog that looked like a Husky walked by with its owner. On the opposite street was a much smaller dog, probably a Shih Tzu, minding its business. The Husky stood attentive and barked loudly as the Shih Tzu prepared to urinate on a tree. Immediately, I felt a kick. I looked at my wife in surprise. As the dog continued to bark, she kicked some more.

"I guess she'll be a dog-lover just like you." My wife knew I loved dogs and planned to get one when the baby was born. I continued to bask in wonder as I felt her tiny limbs creating bulges against the roof of her stomach. She seemed wide awake now!

QUESTIONS AND ANSWERS: WHAT FATHERS NEED TO KNOW

Questions:

1. How much bigger is baby going to get?
2. Can the baby survive if it is born now?
3. What do I do if I hate the name she loves?

214 | JESSE HAYES

Answers:

1. Baby is expected to gain 0.5 to 1 pound per week.
2. At 28 weeks, the baby will be extremely premature but will be able to survive outside the womb. However, there is a risk of permanent disability.
3. Remind your wife that it took both of you to create the baby, therefore you have every right to name the child as well. One of you should take the middle name while the other takes on the first.

8

WADDLE BABY WADDLE BABY— THE EIGHTH MONTH

WEEK TWENTY-NINE

"My wife, who is 8.5 months pregnant, has recently declared herself Mayor of Pillowtown—the sprawling landmass of 7 pillows that currently occupy +75% of our bed. There is no room for me in Pillowtown."

— JONAH LOBE

Your Baby

- **Baby's Growth Spurt:** At 29 weeks, your baby is now the size of a butternut squash. That's a decent size, as the average butternut squash is close to 15.50 inches with a weight of 2.5 to 3 pounds. If you were wondering, 29 weeks is actually 7 months. Only two more months to go! This continues to be a week of intelligence and growth as your baby genius's brain increases in weight, developing the grooves even further to allow for more neurons to surface.

Symptoms to Expect at 29 Weeks

- **Varicose Veins Worsen:** Everything that's happening isn't particularly new, but it can seem worse, and that's because it is. Mom's varicose veins will begin to worsen the closer she gets to the due date. As you're aware, varicose veins have appeared because of an increase in blood volume during the pregnancy as well as those pesky hormones causing her veins to relax. Some women feel extreme pain caused by varicose veins, while others feel nothing at all. Her best bet to curb this symptom is to get exercise and keep her blood circulating.
- **Counting Baby's Kicks:** The doctor may have told mom to begin counting the baby's kicks

every day. This is to be sure that the baby is growing healthily and normally and is remaining as active as they should be. When Mom lies down is when the baby gets active. Doctors recommend at least 10 kicks for an hour, and anything less than 10 kicks in two hours warrants a call to the practitioner.

- **Hemorrhoids, Again:** With the worsening state of the varicose veins, mom can expect her hemorrhoids to also be affected, as they are also considered varicose veins. As mentioned before, lots of fiber-rich foods and fluids are the best ways to combat them.
- **Gassing Up:** Progesterone is back at it again, and it's messing with mom's gastrointestinal tract. Remember that this is the third trimester, and some of the previous symptoms that took a break are now resurfacing. Gas and bloating are examples of that.
- **Keep Mom Active:** No matter how uncomfortable it may seem, it's good to keep mom active. The hormones may be giving her every excuse to want to stay in bed, but that's when she should keep moving all the more. Keep encouraging her that the journey is almost over and that she's doing great! Also, to occupy her time and get prepared, she should consider

applying for maternity leave soon, as there isn't that much time left before the water bag pops!

WEEK THIRTY

Your Baby

- **Size Matters:** We're now at week 30, which means the next 10 weeks are crucial! Your little giant isn't that little anymore and is beginning to take on the personality of the latter name to a greater extent. About the size of a zucchini, the baby weighs close to 3 pounds and is roughly 15.7 inches long. And there's still more to go!
- **30-Week Ultrasound:** If all has been going according to schedule with the pregnancy, unless otherwise directed by the obstetrician, an ultrasound at this time isn't necessary. If you're carrying twins, then the OB might request a biophysical profile for the babies. However, at this time, your baby's skin is getting smoother, and their grip is getting stronger, as baby can now grasp a finger. Soon, it'll be yours!

Symptoms to Expect at 30 Weeks

- **Helping Fight Heartburn:** Heartburn is a symptom, along with gas, that mom may have been struggling with throughout the entire pregnancy. In order to avoid this feeling, avoid serving her any spicy, fried, or acidic foods, especially before bedtime.

- **All About Episiotomies:** No need to worry if this is your first time hearing this word mentioned, but it's definitely worth reading up on. An episiotomy is a procedure that was done traditionally to prevent extensive tearing during childbirth but has been ruled unnecessary in recent years. It involves making an incision in the perineum, which is the tissue between the vaginal opening and the anus. Today, this procedure is still used in specific cases of childbirth, such as if the baby's shoulder is trapped behind Mom's pelvic bone during delivery; if forceps or a vacuum is required; and if the baby's heartrate is seen as abnormal during delivery.

WEEK THIRTY-ONE

Your Baby

- **Coconut-Sized Baby:** Put the lime in the coconut! Your baby is no longer the size of a lime or a lemon but is the size of a coconut! Weighing in at over 3 pounds (closer to 4) and measuring 16 inches, this is what a growth spurt looks like. The more this baby grows, the harder it is to wrap my mind around how something so big can fit … never mind. Let's see their other activities.
- **Sleepy Head:** Mom has probably been noticing longer periods of rest, wakefulness, and activity. That's because the baby has been sleeping much more at this point.
- **Run, Baby, Run:** Your potential track star may already be practicing for the 4 x 400-meter sprint relay as baby's been pedaling their feet more often now. They're deep in concentration and sucking their thumb. Some babies suck their thumbs so voraciously that they're born with a blister!

Symptoms to Expect at 31 Weeks

- **Shortness of Breath:** Mom's uterus has grown and has been positioned at four inches above her belly button. This positioning means that the other organs, like her lungs and diaphragm, are being crowded making it hard to expand fully and breathe. It's likely to remain this way until the baby drops down into the pelvis to prepare for delivery.
- **How Your Baby Responds to Sex:** Not that baby is keenly aware of what's going on around them, but your baby's response to sex might differ depending on their personality. Some aren't affected at all by orgasms and actually fall asleep to the soothing rhythmic motion. Others are excited by the movement and can be stimulated by the action. But this shouldn't stop your lovemaking. You want to keep mom happy and worry less about her present physical condition.
- **Braxton-Hicks:** Who, or what, is Braxton-Hicks? Braxton-Hicks, often referred to as false labor pains, are pregnancy contractions that usually appear during the second and third trimesters. Though uncomfortable, they are not described as painful, but more along the lines of

menstrual cramps. Braxton-Hicks are the way your partner's body prepares for labor.

WEEK THIRTY-TWO

Your Baby

- **As Big as a Cantaloupe:** During week 32, your baby's size development has reached that of a cantaloupe. That's a huge fruit! Their length from crown-to-rump is roughly between 15 and 17 inches, and they weigh between 3.5 and 4 pounds. Baby is getting bigger and bigger for the ultimate date with destiny.
- **Preparing for Birth:** Like an actor preparing for their biggest acting debut, your baby has been honing the thumb-sucking skills necessary to be used on mom's breasts once they're on the outside. She can expect more kicking and pedaling as your little athlete gets their limbs (and mouth) in gear for the outside world. Their skin is also being softened and, as more fat attaches to the baby's body, the less their skin will look transparent and the more they will look like an actual baby.
- **Ultrasound Memory Photos:** With the rise of technology, it's easier than ever to get a 3D or

4D ultrasonogram taken at the mall. That's right! You no longer have to go to a doctor's office to get an ultrasound photo taken. Nevertheless, it's a risk, as the FDA warns that taking ultrasound photos for non-medical reasons and from non-medical sources can expose the baby to more heat from the machine than it will at a doctor's office. Also, qualified technicians are more knowledgeable when it comes to medical equipment than someone at a photography shop. So, you should do what's safest for your spouse and the baby.

Symptoms to Expect at Week 32

- **Hospital Bags, Check:** While 32 weeks may still be too early for anything major to happen, take this time to ensure that the hospital bag for your spouse is already packed and ready to go at a moment's notice, as well as yours. You want her birthing bag to include items such as a copy of her birth plan, health insurance and identification cards, heavy flow sanitary pads, a going-home outfit, newborn diapers and wipes, a nursing pillow, a phone charger, phone, camera, swaddling blankets, slippers, and a few other essentials for the big day. Dads should also have a bag of their own, equipped with many of the same items but also including labor support tools, snacks, and your own change of clothes.

- **The Return of—The Symptoms:** Like a sequel to a scary movie, your partner's first trimester symptoms will be returning about this time. Everything from heartburn and hemorrhoids to insomnia will be coming full circle to assist in this last push before delivery.

THE BABY SHOWER

- **Do Guys Go?** When we look at the pregnancy movies where baby shower scenes are present, we rarely see men in attendance. That's because, traditionally, it has been reserved for ladies and is seen as a time when mothers come together to celebrate the life of a soon-to-be newborn. As more men desire to play an active role in their children's lives, they too want to share in the sending-off ceremony into parenthood. Sure, dads aren't the ones carrying the baby, but if you've been by your partner's side through the emotional rollercoasters and all the other symptoms, you deserve to be recognized for your efforts.

- **What Do Guys Do?** Guys at a baby shower can be similar to guys at a bachelor party, just not as raunchy. They go for many of the same reasons that women go—to support the parents-to-be. There is even the rising popularity of co-ed baby showers, which are joint events for both partners. This is a great way of establishing that both parents will be instrumental in raising their child.

- **Activities to Include:** If it's an all-dad affair, then it'll likely include men getting together, watching sports, and bringing lots of diapers, as most fathers know it's the most coveted item for new fathers. If it's a joint venture with both parents, there are tons of inventive games that both parents can play to make it memorable.

STOCK UP ON ESSENTIALS

When you think of stocking up on essentials before your baby arrives, the thoughts of many tend to linger solely on the obvious, like diapers, wipes, and formula. But there are many other items that are equally important that people often neglect, such as pacifiers, baby bottles, dishwashing liquid, laundry detergent, hand soap, breast milk freezer bags, paper towels, house-cleaning supplies, and disposable diaper bags. If any of these items were not gifted during the baby shower, take the initiative to start stocking up on these items now while there is time.

Let others gift you baby clothes and breast pumps if they so please, but as a dad, the true essentials that you should be focused on are baby diapers, wipes, batteries for the baby monitor, breastmilk storage bags, reusable baby bottles (glass preferably), baby shampoo, petroleum jelly, and baby powder. Above all else, these need to be in place before the baby comes as they will be some of the most frequently used items.

THE PREGNANCY WADDLE

A woman's body is intuitive in so many ways; it prepares her ahead of time for things she doesn't even know she needs. Especially during pregnancy, her body knows exactly what it needs and prepares itself accordingly. However, the very hormonal change that causes her body to be restructured in preparation for the pregnancy is also responsible for 10–25% of pregnancy-related injuries caused by accidental falls, and that is the pregnancy waddle.

The waddle is caused by relaxin, a hormone that loosens the joints and ligaments in her pelvis, causing it to widen ahead of the delivery date and make room for the baby who has been getting into position now. The loosening of her pelvis and the weight being shifted to her front, causes her spine to curve in order to support her back. These changes can cause her gait to be off balance, which is what causes these accidental falls.

You can encourage your spouse to work out those areas of her hips, glutes, and muscles that will best assist her in restoring balance to her walk. She can also try yoga or speak to a physiotherapist who knows exactly what areas of her body need to be worked on.

9

TICKING TIME MOM

"We have a secret in our culture, and it's not that birth is painful. It's that women are strong."

— LAURA STAVOE HARM

WEEK THIRTY-THREE

You're coming down to crunch time as the weeks wane on. There's not much time left once you pass the 37-week mark. Until then, let's see how the baby is progressing.

Your Baby

- **Growing Baby:** At 33 weeks, baby is now the size of a celery stalk, which has a weight and length of 4.2 pounds and over 17 inches, respectively. It's safe to say the baby is coming into their fullness and is still expected to continue growing at a pound a week.
- **Kicks Are Digging deep:** In case you haven't felt it already, your baby's kicks have been feeling like tiny daggers in your partner's uterus. It's not because baby has gotten stronger or more aggressive, but because the amniotic fluid has reached its peak at 33 weeks, so there is less resistance from the fluid, making the baby's kicks feel a bit more intentional.
- **Separating Day From Night:** As the uterine wall thins due to less amniotic fluid in the sac, the early bird now knows when it's morning time to catch the worm. Baby will know the difference between day and night as light can now easily penetrate the womb, causing baby to sleep when it's nighttime and awaken when the sun's up like a normal baby.

Symptoms to Expect at Week 33

- **Pump Mom With Omega-3 Fatty Acids and Calcium:** As the house chef at this time, you should've been incorporating food with omega-3 fatty acids (DHA) from the start of the pregnancy. But in case you have not, it's not too late to start now, as infants born to mothers who have taken omega-3 fatty acids are found to be advanced in their development. DHA is known for enhancing brain and vision development, as well as preventing preterm labor and postpartum depression. But you were warned not to give your wife fish, right? Correct, but raw fish was the emphasis. Well-cooked fish and seafood that is low in mercury can be given a pass, such as shrimp, tilapia, salmon, mackerel, tuna (not bigeye tuna), herring, or sardines. But what if fish is one of her food aversions or she's allergic to fish? Good point. There are alternative sources of DHA, such as flaxseed, chia seed, and walnuts as well as certain brands of eggs, yogurt, soy beverages, and milk. In addition to DHA, ensure that she is getting a healthy dose of calcium, which can be found in milk, cheese, yogurt, broccoli, spinach, and other greens.

WEEK THIRTY-FOUR

Your Baby

- **Baking Bigger in the Oven:** Your little one may not live under the sea or in a pineapple, for that matter, but at thirty-four weeks, he is the size of one. He weighs a cool 5 1/4 pounds and has a length of almost 18 inches. Babies born between weeks 34 and 37 are still considered preterm labor, but if there are no other health problems, they do just as well as full-term babies.
- **Ready for the Ball(s) Drop:** During this week, if your baby is a boy, their testicles will be descending from the abdomen to the scrotum. If, after the baby is born, you don't see their testicles, don't fret. Around 3 to 4% of full-term baby boys are born with undescended testicles, with the drop being completed by their first birthday.

Symptoms to Expect at Week 34

- **Changes in Vision:** There is virtually no organ or bodily function that Mom's hormones don't affect. The same hormones that cause her loose

ligaments can now be affecting her vision,
rendering it blurry at times or hindering
normal tear production, leaving her eyes dry
and irritated. But it's not done screwing with
her eyes yet, as it can cause an increase in fluid
behind the eyes' lenses and make her
temporarily shortsighted or farsighted. But she
won't mind any of these symptoms once she
holds her newborn in her arms.

- **Mom's Swelling Concerns:** Swelling, especially
  in the feet, can be very obvious in pregnant
  women, but it's nothing to be ashamed of. Mom
  is growing together with the baby, which means
  that her growing body tissue will retain fluids.
  The retaining fluids can begin to show up in
  her ankles, feet, and fingers. Try keeping her
  feet elevated so that the fluid can be evenly
  dispersed throughout the body.

- **The Return of Fatigue:** Pregnancy is no walk
  in the park. And especially with the return of
  certain hormone-induced symptoms like
  fatigue, your partner may be feeling down in
  the dumps energetically once again. Between
  shortness of breath, pelvic pain, swollen feet,
  bloating, and gas, sleep is probably hard to
  come by. Try giving her a massage to calm her
  nerves before bedtime or having her drink

soothing teas like chamomile to sleep through the night.

WEEK THIRTY-FIVE

Your Baby

- **Almost Due Honeydew:** With less fluid and space in the uterus, every week leaves your baby with less and less space to move around. What's more, is that baby is now a little over 18 inches in length and is going on 6 pounds. That's a handful of fruit! Speaking of fruit, baby is ripe for the picking, as their limbs are no longer skinny but soft and tender.
- **Baby's Skull Is Soft:** Along with the rest of their body, the baby's brain has also kept growing and developing. However, that brilliant brain's protective armor, the skull, is still soft, and it'll remain that way because a hard, thick skull won't be able to pass through the birth canal. It'll take a total of 18 months after delivery for both the front and back spots of the brain to close and harden completely.

Symptoms to Expect at Week 35

- **Mom's Urination Incontinence:** The constant need to urinate is one thing, but not being able to control it is something entirely different. As you might be suspecting, her hormones are relentless! But not this time. It's actually the baby's head positioned on her bladder that's causing her to need to go all the time. And this time it's worse. It seems that she can't even laugh or sneeze without peeing herself. Wearing a panty liner is a great way to stay prepared for the unexpected.
- **Have You Considered a Doula?** Not to be mistaken with a midwife, although very similar, a doula provides emotional support, and companionship and is trained in breathing and relaxation techniques for labor. The literal translation of the word doula is "woman's servant." Doulas help women to relax during labor and are beside them as a hand to hold. Some women even have less of a need for drugs with a doula by their side.
- **Clumsy Mama:** There are two things that your spouse's body is encountering that are making her clumsy. One is the hormone relaxin that has

caused her joints and ligaments to loosen up, and the other is that her central point of gravity, her belly, is an area of concentrated weight, which is causing her to feel off balance. Encourage her to take every step cautiously at this time, because one wrong leg placement can cause her and the baby serious damage.

- **Install the Baby's Car Seat:** Be forward thinking and try to eliminate any last-minute chaos. While you have the time, install the baby's car seat so you can ride safely.

WEEK THIRTY-SIX

Your Baby

- **Bigger Than Romaine Lettuce:** Feeling cozier in their temporary tiny home, your baby has graduated to the size of a bunch of kale or even a head of romaine lettuce, measuring 18 to 19 inches long and weighing over 6 pounds. Even if baby wants to stay, your baby's growth will drive them to greener pastures outside the comfort of mama's womb.
- **Baby Drops:** The baby's dropping results in lower abdominal pressure, which causes her to

feel a great deal of discomfort in addition to an even greater urge to urinate. The discomfort won't last much longer as the baby's drop is a sign that delivery is around the corner.

- **Weight Gain Acceleration:** Your baby is learning early on the importance of bulking—an ounce per day to be exact. However, the opposite may be happening to their mother at this time.

Symptoms to Expect at Week 36

- **Increased Pelvic Pain:** Mom may want to audition for the Happy Feet trilogy with the penguin waddle she's been sporting! As we know, her hormones have loosened her ligaments and joints a bit, so she's like a walking slinky. However, all this flexibility is causing pelvic pain. Add to that the pressure of the baby's weight dropping onto her pelvis and the weight of the uterus. She deserves a long vacation when this is all done.
- **Decreased Appetite:** While the baby is living their best life and bulking up in weight, mom is having less of a desire to eat, not because she doesn't want to, but because your bambino is

taking up so much space that she can't finish an entire meal. She'll be eating smaller portions more frequently instead, so the baby can continue to be fed.

WHAT IS BREECH?

During the third trimester of pregnancy, usually around week 36, the fetus goes through a position transition in the mother's uterus where the head is pointed downward, facing the vaginal exit so that it is born headfirst. When a baby is breech, however, its positioning is not complete, and it may be left with its feet or buttocks facing the exit. Depending on the position, some breech babies can still be born vaginally, while a C-section is recommended for others.

A few other reasons this may happen are: premature birth, twins, the mother's uterus being abnormally shaped, or there is an abnormal level of amniotic fluid in the uterus.

Besides a C-section, a breech baby can be treated by attempting to re-position the fetus to a head-first posture, or the doctors can prepare for a breech birth, which is a bit trickier.

THE DISCUSSION: BREAST VERSUS BOTTLE

The breast versus bottle debate has been a topic of discussion for decades, but it should be obvious to see why breast will win. First, breast milk is best absorbed by the baby because it was cultivated with the baby in mind, equipped with the balanced amount of nutrients needed to foster the growth of the baby's brain and the development of the nervous system. Studies have found that babies who were breastfed have scored higher on intelligence tests and have better vision. In addition, breast milk helps to protect the baby from mild to severe infections due to the disease-fighting agents that it possesses. As a result, breastfed babies have fewer ear, lung, and digestive infections than formula-fed babies.

On the other hand, formula-fed babies may not be able to fight infections as well and have been found to be more susceptible to such infections well into their adult years. However, there are instances where women simply cannot breastfeed their babies, and that isn't something to be despondent over. Babies fed formula through a bottle grow up to be healthy and strong adults as well. While breastfeeding creates a bond with your child that is truly special, being a parent is more than breastfeeding. So, if, for whatever reason, your spouse is unable to breastfeed, support her in knowing that the most important thing is that the child, boy or girl, has a parent who loves them.

MAKE FREEZER MEALS FOR POST-DELIVERY

Prepping meals ahead of time makes all the difference, especially after a tiring child delivery! You want to ensure that your prepping contains a balanced blend of vitamins and minerals that'll be ideal for a mother regaining strength from labor and passing those nutrients onto a newborn baby. These dishes must be able to help her produce enough breast milk to continuously feed the baby and even do some breast pumping to store away milk for the baby as well.

According to the prenatal nutritionist Ryann Kipping, postpartum freezer meals should contain vitamins A, D, and K; choline; and the omega-3 fatty acid DHA, which is an essential part of their nutritional makeup. Don't forget high protein foods like beef, pork, chicken, vegetable soup, eggs, broth, and fish. You want to freeze meals that are nutritious, easy to make, and easy to warm up. Not only that, but if you and your partner recently invested a ton of money into baby essentials, you're trying to save any way you can. And buying (healthy) takeout every day seems counterproductive for someone looking to save for the future. Trust me, it's much cheaper to buy and cook your own food for storage.

With that said, here are a few simple meals that are cheap to make then freeze and are easy to heat up:

- casseroles
- soups, stews, and broths
- meatballs
- seasoned meat (chicken, beef, pork, fish)
- breaded chicken
- bread
- lasagna
- slow cooked meats
- smoothie packets
- homemade frozen pizza

Also, if your spouse is extremely cautious about the food she eats, which she should be with the baby, there are succulent paleo and gluten-free meals that will complement that lifestyle. The possibilities are truly endless when it comes to preparing these types of foods, so don't be afraid to get creative with your meal preps.

☆ YOU HAVE TO KNOW LOVE TO SHOW LOVE: A PERSONAL STORY

One of the main things I wanted myself and my wife to work on before bringing this innocent soul into our lives was the way in which we love ourselves and others. It took me a few bad relationships, some of them even with people I had known and loved as a child, to know that in order to show love, you have to know love for yourself.

Before deciding we wanted to bring our own baby into the world, I wanted us to be sure we knew what it was to even love ourselves. So, we spent a few days doing things to better ourselves. I encouraged my wife to spend some time exercising and meditating. We're both into prayer and meditation as well, so I encouraged her to spend a good amount of time praying and asking God for his will to be done regarding the pregnancy. This was the first child for both of us, and I thought we should both be in the best place mentally, physically, and spiritually to welcome this new life into our world.

This wasn't a self-love journey for her only, though. I also took the time to pray and ask for direction in becoming a father. No parent is actually given a manual on how to be a successful parent. I think I once read a small 71-page book called *Successful Fathers: The Subtle but Powerful Ways Fathers Mold Their Children's Characters*, which was one of the best things I've ever done for self-love and self-improvement. I understood that in order to give our children the best in life, we needed to want the best for ourselves. Therefore, we both need to stop habits of self-destruction, such as eating unhealthy foods and not taking the best care of our bodies through exercise.

QUESTIONS AND ANSWERS: WHAT FATHERS NEED TO KNOW

Questions:

1. Can I convince my partner to breastfeed?
2. What if I pass out in the delivery room?

Answers:

1. Your wife may not be feeling confident about her ability to provide milk. It can be because of her breast size or just being intimidated by the size of a baby bottle. Encourage her that a baby's stomach is no bigger than a walnut and that she will have more than enough. Allow her

to voice her opinions and inspire her to give it a shot.

2. Let someone know immediately if you are feeling faint. You also want to find a chair to sit in with your head between your knees, as this helps blood circulate to your brain.

10

YES, SHE'S STILL PREGNANT

Contrary to popular belief, pregnancy lasts longer than 9 months. Doctors usually consider a woman pregnant after the fourth week of pregnancy because that is around the time she sees her period. That is because the physical signs of pregnancy are much easier to spot, but at one week pregnant, she may only be exhibiting signs of a normal menstrual cycle, involving cramps and vaginal bleeding. Nothing too special. So, when the pregnancy test shows positive for pregnancy, your partner has been pregnant for four weeks already, which explains why the pregnancy may seem to go on for longer than expected. So, remember that it's not always that the baby is overdue; you may have been given a calculation that was off by a couple weeks.

WEEK THIRTY-SEVEN

Your Baby

- **Baby Is the Size of a Swiss Chard:** Surely, your baby isn't dreaming about this, but at 37 weeks he is the size of a bundle of Swiss chard. Now that you're so much closer to being full-term, your baby measures 19 inches in length and a whopping 6.68 pounds and is still considered "early-term." Baby won't be seen as full-term until 39 weeks, so hang in there!
- **Head and Body Is Fattening:** For as big as your baby's head is, there must be the brains of a genius-in-the-making. Their head is huge and is continuing to grow, in addition to their shoulders, elbows, hips, and knees—baby is going to be a plump pumpkin in a few short weeks!
- **Practice Makes Perfect:** Ambition and determination will be their middle names because your little achiever is still practicing the suck and swallow technique with the amniotic fluid. Baby is also sucking their thumb and blinking in preparation for all the world has to offer.

Symptoms to Expect at Week 37

- **Dilating a Bit Early?** Dilation is the process by which your wife's cervix must be opened by at least 10 centimeters, which will allow the baby to pass into the birth canal. The practitioner will first check for the ripeness of your partner's cervix and then for effacement, or the thinness of her cervix. This process can take days to weeks or a month to reach full dilation before knowing the baby is ready for delivery.
- **What's a Perineal Massage?** While it sounds like a fancy spa treatment, it's far from it. A perineal massage is done to help stretch the area of the skin between the vagina and rectum, which helps to avoid vaginal tearing and the "stinging" sensation the baby may cause during crowning.

WEEK THIRTY-EIGHT

Your Baby

- **The Size of a Mini Watermelon:** Your little one isn't so little anymore; baby weighs about 7 pounds and measures 20 inches in length—they are now compared to a mini-watermelon! From a raspberry to a 7-pound fruit is remarkable progress. The lanugo is also shedding just in time for their arrival, but some babies are still born with some lanugo left at times.

Symptoms to Expect at Week 38

- **Leaking Breasts:** Here's a little surprise neither of you may have been expecting—leaking breasts. Yes, your partner's breasts may have begun to leak a yellow liquid substance called colostrum, which is a precursor to mom's breast milk. Colostrum is actually full of protein and has less fat and sugar than breast milk, but it probably doesn't taste as good to the baby either. If she hasn't already, suggest that she wear breast pads in her bra to avoid her clothes getting dirty. This is something she will have to get used to.
- **Distractions During Labor:** In order to help your spouse block out the pain and other forms of discomfort, there are a few distractions that can help. A few of these distractions include music; a tennis ball, stress ball, or other item to hold or squeeze; breathing patterns; visualization; meditation; prayer; playing an instrument; candy; or even ice.

- **Get Mom to Do Squats:** Even at thi
  in the pregnancy, you should still b
  encouraging your partner to exerc
  hasn't been doing so herself. Have her
  incorporate squats into her workout routine as
  they have been known to speed up labor by
  increasing the pelvic opening so the baby can
  easily descend.
- **Feed Her Labor-Inducing Foods:** Not every
  age-old adage about methods to induce labor
  actually works. But there may be an element of
  truth when it comes to labor-inducing foods. A
  few well-known foods to eat right before your
  due date are eggplant, pineapple, dates,
  balsamic vinegar, spicy food, castor oil, and red
  raspberry leaf tea.

WEEK THIRTY-NINE

Your Baby

- **The Baby Is Full-term!** Your little pumpkin is
  now the actual size of a pumpkin at 39 weeks.
  Your baby now measures 19 to 21 inches with a
  weight of 7 to 8 pounds. It's funny that their
  head accounts for one third of that weight.
  Enjoy this last bit of time with your partner and

the baby in the womb, because at any moment it can be go time!

Symptoms to Expect at Week 39

- **Be Watchful for Signs of Labor:** There are a few unmistakable signs that your partner has gone into labor that you should be looking out for.

1. The main sign is strong contractions that last between 30 and 70 seconds and recur 5 to 10 minutes apart. These are not to be confused with Braxton-Hicks, as they are much stronger and more intense. The closer the baby gets to crowning, the stronger and closer together the birth pains become.
2. Your spouse may also experience an unrelenting and unwavering pain in her lower back and belly, which counts as a sign of labor.
3. If at 39 weeks your spouse complains of a brownish or reddish vaginal discharge, this can also be a tell-tale sign she is going into labor.
4. A popular sign of going into labor is the breaking of the water bag (the amniotic sac that the baby has been housed in for over 9 months). When the bags tear, she may feel a gush of

water or a trickle down her leg that isn't her incontinence urination.

- **Preparing for a C-Section:** If your wife has to have a C-Section (cesarean section), she needs to first prepare by signing a surgery consent form and speaking to her doctor about her diet and birthing plan in the weeks leading up to the procedure. She is to eat or drink nothing for eight hours prior to the C-Section, except 8 ounces of apple juice. Two hours before the surgery, she should take nothing by mouth. The evening before and the morning of the surgery, she must use 2 Chlorhexidine Gluconate (CHG) wipes after bathing. She must also stop all medications before the surgery.

WEEK FORTY

Your Baby

- **Behold, the Newborn Baby:** There really is nothing left to compare your child to except a healthy, kicking, thumb-sucking newborn! Like any other newborn, they weigh about 6 to 9 pounds and average a length of between 19 and 22 inches. No sweat if baby is a little smaller or bigger than these figures. They're still a healthy champion.

- **Skin Color Expectations:** No matter the ethnicity of your spouse or yourself, all babies are born with a reddish-purple tinge that changes to pinkish red a few days after. Because the baby's skin is still thin, the blood vessels are easily visible, giving it a pink tint. Only over the next six months after birth will your baby have a permanent skin color.

Symptoms to Expect at Week 40

- **Will Her Water Break?** If your partner is anxious over when and how her water will break, assure her that it's nothing like what you see in the movies. Most of the time, it's a slow trickle or a small gush and isn't that dramatic. Another lie Hollywood made you believe is that almost every woman begins labor with her amniotic bag breaking, when only 15% of women experience a rupture before labor.
- **Can Sex Induce Labor?** Here's another old adage that keeps moms and dads busy making babies: sex can induce labor. According to a 2006 study from the National Library of Medicine, couples who were sexually active

tended to deliver much sooner than those who were not. In that case, you can keep rocking the boat all through the pregnancy!

- **Frustration in the Wait?** Missed due dates can seem a bit discouraging and downright frustrating, but it's common for calculated due dates to be missed. Depending on when her last period was before impregnation, she may not be as late as she thinks. Stay positive, and before you know it, she'll be in the delivery room.

WHAT HAPPENS IF THE BABY IS PAST DUE?

Some babies find it too cozy in mom's tummy. And while they may not find a problem with being past due, they definitely create a scare and lots of anxiety for those waiting on the delivery. It's important to note that putting your hope on a due date can leave you disappointed because it doesn't estimate exactly when the baby will arrive. It's actually normal to give birth past the due date. As a matter of fact, only 1 in 20 women delivers on the actual due date given by their obstetrician. A pregnancy must continue for two weeks past the due date to be considered a post term pregnancy. So, don't fret because you're a few days off the target. There's really no danger to the mother or the child.

An overdue baby may look a bit different than a baby born before the due date or on the day itself. They may appear with peeling skin, extended arms and legs, or longer hair and nails than normal babies. Post term babies have also been found to be extremely alert at the moment of their birth, supposedly from being in the womb for extra time with their eyes open.

Overdue pregnancies are not without the risk of danger, however. Some of the risks associated with post term pregnancies include:

- stillbirth
- macrosomia
- post maturity syndrome (dysmaturity)
- severe vaginal tearing
- infection
- postpartum bleeding

Also, here are some reasons to consider why you may be experiencing a post term pregnancy. I assure you, it's not always as bad as you believe:

- This is your first pregnancy.
- Your baby is a boy.
- You have a history of overdue pregnancy.
- You are obese (body mass index of 30 or higher).

WHAT TO KNOW ABOUT BEING INDUCED

While a natural birth is always to be expected, we also need to remain realistic about the possibility of something going wrong and labor having to be induced. There are certain prerequisites that allow for induced labor, and one of those is if your spouse is significantly past her due date. We're talking more than two weeks past the expected date. The California-based OBGYN, Dr. Colleen Wittenberg, stated that induction is also advised if the placenta is failing or the amniotic fluid is too low. Induction is a tedious process, much like the entire pregnancy process, and can take hours or a few days depending on the cervical exam results. Once the induction takes place, the baby is usually born within the next 24 hours. Let's look at a few particulars surrounding induced labor and what you can expect if ever it were to be suggested by a doctor.

- **Labor Induction Stimulates Contractions:** When a woman doesn't go into labor naturally, labor induction is considered an artificial starter through medical intervention. However, the process is mostly avoided unless the mother or baby is in a compromising state.
- **Induction Is Done Only When Necessary:** There are only a few instances that will make

labor induction necessary. Some of these include:

1. The baby is overdue by two weeks.
2. Complications make natural delivery dangerous (heart disease, bleeding, gestational diabetes, hypertension, preeclampsia).
3. More than 24–48 hours have passed since the amniotic sac ruptured and labor has not started.
4. An infection known as chorioamnionitis is present inside the uterus.
5. The baby isn't receiving sufficient nutrients and oxygen from the placenta.

WHAT TO EXPECT DURING BIRTH

As her partner, there are certain signs you will need to be aware of during labor just in case your spouse may have missed them. It helps to know that she has someone dependable who is just as alert and expectant as she is. Some of these signs we have already listed in the previous chapters, such as her water breaking, a dull, achy pain in her lower back similar to menstrual aches, regularly increasing contractions with shorter time intervals in between, or passing the mucus plug in her cervical canal.

Now that you know the labor signs to look for, it'll be helpful to know the ways in which you can help your partner once labor has begun. You can also inform the delivery team of some of your methods so you can jump in to assist at the right time. Here are a few ways you can comfort your spouse:

- Help her to release stress by massaging her temples.
- Remind her to urinate if she has to, since a full bladder can stall labor.
- Use cool compresses on her neck and face to keep her feeling good.
- If the doctor allows it, keep her hydrated and energized with healthy fluids and snacks as she continues in labor.
- Help to change her position to progress the labor naturally.
- Use your hand to apply pressure on her back to help relieve some of her back pain.
- Apply a heated pad or warm blanket to the areas she is experiencing pain.
- Make the baby her motivation so she remains focused on the mission of delivery.

WHAT IF SHE HAS A C-SECTION?

If a C-section is a matter of necessity rather than an option, you can still play an instrumental role alongside your wife every step of the way. You can even relay some of her wishes to the doctors if the entire process becomes too stressful and tiring for her. If a C-section is required, you can stay with her in the operating room once the doctor allows it. It's usually permitted unless she needs a general anesthetic.

For hygiene purposes, dad will be given a medical hat, top, and trousers to put on before entering the operating room. Once your partner is settled into the OR, you will be allowed to stand behind her head behind a partition that separates you and your wife while the doctors get to work on the other side.

Once the C-section has been successfully completed, it takes at least 6 weeks to recover, although feelings of discomfort may last for much longer than that. During her time of rest and recovery at home, you can help her by:

- Help her get in and out of bed.
- Take over all the heavy lifting from her.
- Remind her to take her pain medications.
- Give her the newborn to cuddle and play with.

- Give her emotional support.
- Feed the baby with expressed breast milk or baby formula.
- Change the baby's diaper.
- Do housecleaning.
- Do the shopping.

☆ LET'S JUST HAVE SEX, ALREADY: A PERSONAL STORY

"I feel like a walking trauma room. My ankles are swollen, I have severe back pain, I can't laugh without sprinkling myself, and my emotions are all over the place," my wife complained as we walked along the secluded beach. I wanted to take her away from the home and the city and celebrate something like a babymoon. We never really got a chance to enjoy our own honeymoon after we got married because we both had such demanding careers. But with our first baby on the way, I figured why not kill two birds with one stone.

"I'd be lying if I said I understand exactly what you're going through because I don't. I can only say that it's not going to last forever. While we're both dealing with it, let's try our best to enjoy this time together … with our unborn baby." I added to change the emotional state she was in. "Pregnancy looks good on you, anyway. I enjoy seeing you waltz around like an umpa-lumpa," I remarked with a teasing smile.

"You don't know how it is, honey. I just want the baby to come out, already. I feel like there's so much I want to do … but there's this huge bowling ball in front of me. Do you know that I can no longer see my toes?" She asked, almost in disbelief. We had walked almost the entire stretch of the beach and had reached a hidden cave toward the far end. We were about to turn back when I heard, "I can't wait any longer. I want to have sex right now … right here! On the beach!"

I looked puzzled. "Huh? Where did this come from?" I asked in confusion. Our sex life was on a rollercoaster ride, and I blamed her emotions for it. "Let's just wait until we get back to the house," I suggested.

"No. That's just it. As much as I love this baby and the idea of being a mother soon, I miss our spontaneous love life. That's why I can't wait to give birth. I miss the things we used to do…" she explained while slowly unbuckling my belt. "There's no one around, honey. Let's get a head start on how our love life used to be!"

With that statement, I was smitten. "Alright. It seems those hormones are acting up again. Well … you asked for it. Now let's dance." You'd be surprised at what a little privacy in a beach cave can do for your love life.

QUESTIONS AND ANSWERS: WHAT FATHERS NEED TO KNOW

Questions:

1. How long after birth can we have sex again?
2. I'm really scared about being a dad. What if I am bad at it?

Answers:

1. Health practitioners recommend waiting at least four to six weeks after delivery to have sex with your partner. This is to avoid any complications that may arise from having sex too soon after giving birth.
2. Fatherhood can be both thrilling and intimidating. You are useful in many ways and that usefulness can be shown beginning during pregnancy. While being a father is a huge responsibility, it doesn't help to think that you have to transform into a police officer to raise your family. Of course, you want to take charge and set an example, but you are still allowed to have a little fun as well.

11

CALL ME "DADDY"—THE FIRST 11 MONTHS WITH A BABY

"Never is a man more a man than when he is the father of a newborn."

— MATTHEW MCCONAUGHEY

THE FIRST MONTH

The storm is over now, and the baby and your spouse are both home and safe in your care. This is the calm after the storm, though, as all seems peaceful and simple right now. The baby may only want food (breastmilk) every few hours, sleep, and a diaper change every now and then. While things are this simple, enjoy them. Take the opportunity to do laundry and as many household chores as possible, as things will get more complicated in the coming weeks!

You're a first-time dad with no schedule or handbook given to you. During the first month, you want to work on establishing a routine around the house while keeping up with the baby's nutrition and breastfeeding. Ensure that mom is well fed to produce the baby's food and try to get at least some rest. You'll also want to make time to swaddle your baby and bond with her, if it's a girl.

The bulk of the pressure may be on you for some time, but it's not going to last forever. Once your wife is properly healed, you two can establish a routine around the house so that no one feels overwhelmed. And when it comes to feeding, whether your baby prefers boobs or the bottle, you can help out your spouse by comforting her in her new role as a mother.

- **Bonding:** Part of the bonding process is to learn your baby's cues. They can't speak just yet, so through sounds and cries is how they'll be able to get their point across. Also, bonding allows mom some time to rest and produce more milk after feedings if she's breastfeeding. Connect with your baby through touch and talking. You're also going to establish who you are in their lives by doing so. You can take over from mom by bathing the baby, picking them up when they cry, dressing them, or playing with them.

- **Helping Mom:** Mom will be the go-to source for the baby for a while after birth. They've already built a tight bond from the womb, and now she is food! The baby will obviously be stuck on mom, which will tire her eventually. For all her hard work, let her know that she's doing a great job. Tell her how much you love her and how she's already proving to be a great mother. Let her vent to you and listen to what she has to say without any judgment. She will need the emotional support after what she's been through.

THE SECOND MONTH

During the second month, your baby is still building up coordination and reflexes, but doesn't have enough to hold objects like toys as yet. By this time, you and your baby are beginning to bond more, and you're learning more about their personality and the things that make them tick. You will also be noticing what different cries mean—whether it's a dirty diaper that needs changing, hunger, or wanting to sleep. Their personality will begin to come forth, and you'll know exactly what they want.

- **Second Month Milestones:** Your baby's sleep patterns may also be better understood at 2 months. They can sleep for 15 to 16 hours a day in sporadic intervals. This means they may not be able to sleep through the night just yet, especially breastfed babies who wake up every three or four hours for food.

- **Eating and Pooping:** Life is fairly simple for your newborn because they only have to eat and poop. Eating may happen every 3 to 4 hours with even longer streaks at night. Encourage Mom to use the breast pump and storage bags to store extra in the freezer. This way, instead of waking her up constantly, you can grab a bag of milk and feed the baby yourself. This will result in a healthy dose of soft and slightly runny diapers, at least 4 to 6 per day. The stool should never be red, black, or white.

- **Developing Senses:** Baby's five senses are also developing at this time, but they have a way to go. They can see people and objects from up to 18 inches away and are able to follow you around the room with their eyes. However, they will be recognizing you and your partner's faces more clearly, especially as you draw closer to baby for feeding.

- **Communication Methods:** As stated, the default method of communication is crying at 2 months of age. But baby may also be cooing, grunting, and gurgling with spontaneous noises at times. While communication skills may be limited, it's important that you and your partner speak to baby. The more you speak, the more your little one will recognize your voices, which will encourage them to start forming words in a few months.

- **Smell, Taste, and Touch:** Baby's sense of smell, taste, and touch are all growing stronger at this moment. They will be reaching for things to touch, so giving baby a few colorful toys will keep them occupied and train them to better hold things. Your baby also enjoys sweet smells like any other adult will. The same can be said for baby's sense of taste—sweet over bitter any day!

THE THIRD MONTH

As you can see, growth has only seemed to speed up since leaving the womb. At three months, your infant's motor skills are growing and developing ever more right now. Their upper-body strength should have increased, enabling baby to hold their head up with their arms and chest when laying on their stomach. They will also be doing the "superman" where they lie on their stomach and lift both their legs and hands in the air. This will also strengthen their legs. Baby's hand-eye coordination should also have improved since last month; they are now able to close and open their hands and briefly grab a toy rattle.

- **Third Month Milestones:** Sleep patterns have improved as your baby has settled down to sleep for a stretch of six or seven hours at a time. If your baby cries during the night, don't be too in a rush to pick them up, as they will usually go back to sleep after a few seconds. They will soon come to understand that nighttime is for sleep only.
- **Senses:** If you're playing music around your little one, they are most likely smiling and looking around, displaying signs of enjoyment. You may also recognize these smiles whenever

they hear your voice. Their eye contact is also strengthening, and they will stare at you when you hold them. Do your due diligence and take the time to speak to your baby, as studies have shown that parents who speak to their children continuously have them grow up to have a better understanding of social behaviors, better conversational skills, and the ability to grasp vocabulary very well.

- **Exploring the Outside World:** At some point, you'll want to take your little one out of the house and into nature. This is also a great way to bond and communicate even more. The house scenery may be getting a bit stale as well, so a walk in the stroller is an excellent way to keep their curious mind satisfied. However, this does take preparation, so ensure that you have all the essentials in case of an emergency.

RECONNECTING WITH YOUR SPOUSE

You and your spouse might have made it over the hurdle of delivering your baby, but now there's something else that needs a new birth, and that's your relationship. It's easy to get so carried away with the needs of the baby and them being the focus of attention that you and your partner begin to drift apart, which neither of you really wants. You're both extremely tired and overworked following the pregnancy and, most recently, the delivery. Your spouse went from the pain and triumph of giving birth to being thrust into late nights of breastfeeding or formula feeding a hungry newborn. You are probably feeling stretched as well and have continued to take on the bulk of all the housework, cooking, cleaning, and preparing. So, you're both understandably and noticeably tired. But as things begin to settle down, how do you reconnect with your spouse? Here are a few tips to get the ship sailing again:

- **Listen to Your Partner:** A busy life is an understatement when it comes to you and your spouse. If you've gone back to work after the baby, that means she is mostly at home tending to the baby. When you get home, she may be asleep, and you will have to feed the baby. It's a serious balancing act that may leave no time for the two of you to spend together. Even if you're out working to provide, it may feel frustrating on her end to know that you're gone all day and she's alone with the baby. Speaking openly and honestly about your feelings right now is key. You may be able to lend your support if you are aware of exactly what's going on beneath the surface with your spouse. Maybe you can offer to prepare food for her for the week so she doesn't have to cook every day. Communicate your concerns to each other to better find a solution.

- **Share Responsibilities:** The home duties may have doubled, but your bickering shouldn't. After a baby, finances may be tight, time may be limited, and tensions may flare. Delegating tasks between the two of you should help to calm the noise and get to work on maintaining peace in the household and in your marriage. When you do have the extra time, don't hesitate to chip in and do things like bathe the baby if she hasn't yet or wash the dishes if they've mounted up—do things to help the situation.

- **Go On a Date:** When was the last time the two of you had a date night? Having a baby isn't the end of the world and doesn't have to be the end of your relationship. As a matter of fact, it needs to be stronger now so that your baby can grow up with both their parents. That's why it's important to invest in each other by taking your spouse out to her favorite restaurant. Do the things you used to do before the baby came to keep things exciting. And don't forget to be spontaneous (not suggesting you be in a rush to carelessly get pregnant again). Being parents

doesn't mean you should neglect your
relationship with each other.

- **Keep the Fire Burning:** Stress and worry are
  two negative emotions that, if displayed
  regularly, can cause a couple to call it quits.
  That's why it's necessary to make time for
  yourselves and for each other. If she met you
  when you were in shape, get back to doing just
  that. Hit the gym again, re-commit to your
  daily runs, or do a set of workouts to keep
  yourself trim. You must maintain the attraction
  and her interest so that the spark remains alive
  and well. This way, will be no issues in the
  bedroom as you will both be feeling your best,
  despite being parents.

☆ STARTING BACK AT ONE: A PERSONAL STORY

Having a baby with my wife was one of the biggest
moments in my life, and there were no regrets with that
one, at all! It's what happened after that had me second-
guessing even starting a family with her in the first
place. Life was so packed now that we barely had time
for each other. It was so bad that even sex was
becoming more of a chore than a desire. But I planned
to change that with a dinner at our favorite seafood
restaurant. Hopefully, this would turn things around.

"Where are you taking me now?" asked my wife. I had her close her eyes while I drove to the first place I took her when we began dating. She has wanted to eat there almost every weekend since—she said the breaded coconut shrimp had her hooked.

"You'll see ... Its's a place that you should *smell* in the distance." I responded in a suspenseful voice.

"Smell?" Oh God, honey ... where are you taking me?" she asked nervously.

"Just relax, we're almost there." I replied eagerly.

When we arrived and she uncovered her eyes, I could tell she was alight with excitement. "We haven't been here in forever! Oh my gosh! How did you remember? This has been our favorite food spot since ... forever!" She giggled. "I hope they still have the breaded shrimp with the Carbonara sauce. That really used to hit the spot," she said, peering into my eyes. "I'm really glad you brought me here, baby. I really needed this. Better yet ... we really needed this."

"Yea, I know. You've been so busy with the baby, and I've been pulling double shifts at work—it's just been crazy. But tonight, is our night. I got us a reservation under the gazebo. Just you and me," I concluded as I caressed the curve of her hip. I felt her body shiver. I knew it was going to be a good night.

We ordered our meals, drank two bottles of her favorite white wine, and ate lots of breaded shrimp. I could see that she was back in her element—jovial, witty, funny, and seductive. Of course, we didn't forget to check in on the baby, who was keeping her parents on their toes. All is well that ends well, and I can assure you, the night ended well.

QUESTIONS AND ANSWERS: WHAT FATHERS NEED TO KNOW

Questions:

1. Does she love our child more than she loves me?
2. How do I know if the baby loves me?

Answers:

1. After birth and for years thereafter, children tend to take center stage almost all the time. It may even seem like your partner loves your child more than you. Children shower you with affection, so they're easier to love. But adult relationships are more complex and require more compromise as your lives are split

between home, work, children, your own hobbies, and each other.

2. Babies have their own love language, like any other person does. If your baby stares into your eyes, smiles at you, tries talking to you, or wants you around, then these are sure-fire signs that they love you.

CONCLUSION

Pregnancy is a beautiful, confusing, terrifying, and exhilarating process that any father will be proud to have been a part of. If you're one of the fathers who endeavors to stick around for your baby for years to come, then you will be thrilled to be investing in them from day one. Now that you're a father, you are aware of what it means to take responsibility for your actions, whether they were planned or happened spontaneously. If anything at all, the pregnancy process will teach you to have greater respect for women and the pain they experience shortly after the pleasure they get into bed for. Despite the arguments that may arise along the way, loving the person who gave birth to an extension of yourself is a huge blessing that is often forgotten in today's culture. Too many people get into relationships for the wrong reasons and leave at the worst times, like when a baby is on the way. After reading this book, you should have a better understanding of the amount of pain, sacrifice, and discomfort a woman goes through to give birth to a single child.

Becoming a father will also challenge your perception of what a man's role is in a relationship. I'm not saying that a man should completely abandon their role as the masculine figure in their relationship or family, but the process of pregnancy should teach you that it won't hurt to pick up a broom and sweep the floor or wash the dishes if your wife is not in the position to do so. Perhaps she used to cater to you before—make you breakfast, cook dinner, do your laundry, and fold your clothes—but when she is pregnant, the dynamics are slightly reversed. And you should embrace this temporary reverse whole-heartedly because not only is it temporary, but you're doing a service for your family.

If you were formerly careless with finances, then maybe a baby is exactly what you needed to regain your focus and help you prioritize your life. Grown people do grown things, and having a baby is as grown as it gets. Remember that any MALE can impregnate a woman, but it takes a MAN to stick around and raise a family. You will no longer be short-sighted, but you will begin to prepare for the future. Getting life insurance, building a college fund for your child, taking steps to create generational wealth, and saving for the retirement of you and your partner are all ways in which you can step up to the plate and begin being a man. You will now have more mouths to feed. You want to ensure that you are doing your best to make life as comfortable for them as possible.

This book is designed to equip you not only with knowledge for handling a 40-week pregnancy but also for life after the baby is born. You should strive to be the best father you can be and the best husband that you can be. Pregnancy should also teach you that life isn't always going to go smoothly, but that doesn't mean it can't be beautiful. You just witnessed your lovely spouse endure months of morning sickness, cramps, headaches, backaches, dizziness, and disorientation only to birth a beautiful human being at the end of it all. So that lets you know that even in pain and distress, there is beauty and purpose. You can now implement this knowledge and become the best version of yourself as a man and as a romantic partner.

Besides being responsible, mature, and financially sound, you also should have learned to be sacrificial. As a teenager and young adult, you might have led a selfish life, not thinking of the consequences of your actions or the impact of your choices. But you should've learned that life is about being of service to others, which denotes a certain sense of selflessness. Think about it. It takes a level of selflessness to avoid smoking, drinking, and clubbing with your friends to stay at home with your wife while she is pregnant. It took selflessness to keep the house clean, cook for her, and massage her back and her feet for her when you could have been doing anything else besides that. And rest assured, it will take that same level of selflessness to be a father.

So, congratulations, dad! You have graduated to another level in the school of life. It's impossible to give you everything you need to know in this book, as some things you will learn on your own while continuing along your journey. You can even keep this safe and pass it on to your son, nephew, cousin, or friend who is also on their way to becoming a "Virgin Dad."

If you enjoyed the contents of this book, feel free to leave a review to help other first-time dads on their quest to become better men, spouses, and fathers. Thanks for reaching this far!

To leave a quick review just scan the QR code below!

REFERENCES

1 week pregnant. (2022, June 8). TheBUMP. https://www.thebump.com/pregnancy-week-by-week/1-weeks-pregnant

10 weeks pregnant. (2022, June 8). TheBUMP. https://www.thebump.com/pregnancy-week-by-week/10-weeks-pregnant

Berry-Johnson, J. (2018, June 27). *11 financial moves every new parent should make*. Forbes. https://www.forbes.com/sites/janetberryjohnson/2018/06/27/11-financial-moves-every-new-parent-should-make/

CDC-Centers for Disease Control and Prevention. (2020, September 18). *Toxoplasmosis: Pregnancy FAQS*. CDC. https://www.cdc.gov/parasites/toxoplasmosis/gen_info/pregnant.html

Donaldson-Evans, C. (2021a, June 24). *Week 4 of pregnancy*. What to Expect. https://www.whattoexpect.com/pregnancy/week-by-week/week-4.aspx

Donaldson-Evans, C. (2021b, June 24). *Week 6 of pregnancy*. What to Expect. https://www.whattoexpect.com/pregnancy/week-by-week/week-6.aspx

Donaldson-Evans, C. (2021c, June 24). *Week 7 of pregnancy*. What to Expect. https://www.whattoexpect.com/pregnancy/week-by-week/week-7.aspx

Donaldson-Evans, C. (2021d, June 24). *Week 8 of pregnancy*. What to Expect. https://www.whattoexpect.com/pregnancy/week-by-week/week-8.aspx

Donaldson-Evans, C. (2021e, June 24). *Week 9 of pregnancy*. What to Expect. https://www.whattoexpect.com/pregnancy/week-by-week/week-9.aspx

Donaldson-Evans, C. (2021f, June 24). *Week 10 of pregnancy*. What to Expect. https://www.whattoexpect.com/pregnancy/week-by-week/week-10.aspx

Donaldson-Evans, C. (2021g, June 24). *Week 11 of pregnancy*. What to

Expect. https://www.whattoexpect.com/pregnancy/week-by-week/week-11.aspx

Donaldson-Evans, C. (2021h, June 24). *Week 13 of pregnancy*. What to Expect. https://www.whattoexpect.com/pregnancy/week-by-week/week-13.aspx

Donaldson-Evans, C. (2021i, June 24). *Week 14 of pregnancy*. What to Expect. https://www.whattoexpect.com/pregnancy/week-by-week/week-14.aspx

Donaldson-Evans, C. (2021j, June 24). *Week 15 of pregnancy*. What to Expect. https://www.whattoexpect.com/pregnancy/week-by-week/week-15.aspx

Donaldson-Evans, C., & Wu, J. (2021, June 24). *Week 5 of pregnancy*. What to Expect. https://www.whattoexpect.com/pregnancy/week-by-week/week-5.aspx

Downs, M. (2009, February 5). *An expectant dad's guide to pregnancy*. WebMD. https://www.webmd.com/baby/features/an-expectant-dads-guide-to-pregnancy

Durocher, G. (2020, April 30). *My wife is pregnant! Now what?* Safe Ride 4 Kids. https://saferide4kids.com/blog/wife-is-pregnant/

Family Education Staff. (2019, May 15). *6 ways to make your pregnant partner feel sexy—Familyeducation*. Family Education. https://www.familyeducation.com/family-life/6-ways-make-your-pregnant-partner-feel-sexy

Gates, M. (2022a, March 10). *6 weeks pregnant*. BabyCenter. https://www.babycenter.com/pregnancy/week-by-week/6-weeks-pregnant

Gates, M. (2022b, March 10). *7 weeks pregnant*. BabyCenter. https://www.babycenter.com/pregnancy/week-by-week/7-weeks-pregnant

Gates, M. (2022c, March 10). *8 weeks pregnant*. BabyCenter. https://www.babycenter.com/pregnancy/week-by-week/8-weeks-pregnant

Gates, M. (2022d, March 21). *11 weeks pregnant*. BabyCenter. https://www.babycenter.com/pregnancy/week-by-week/11-weeks-pregnant

Gates, M. (2022e, March 22). *12 weeks pregnant.* BabyCenter. https://www.babycenter.com/pregnancy/week-by-week/12-weeks-pregnant

Gates, M. (2022f, March 24). *13 weeks pregnant.* BabyCenter. https://www.babycenter.com/pregnancy/week-by-week/13-weeks-pregnant

Gates, M. (2022g, March 30). *15 weeks pregnant.* BabyCenter. https://www.babycenter.com/pregnancy/week-by-week/15-weeks-pregnant

Johnson, A. (2017, February 3). *9 first trimester red flags to keep an eye on.* Romper. https://www.romper.com/p/9-first-trimester-red-flags-you-shouldnt-ignore-34633

Lewsley, J. (n.d.). *How do I handle my partner's mood swings?* BabyCentre UK. https://www.babycentre.co.uk/a1011720/how-do-i-handle-my-partners-mood-swings

Mann, D. (2022, March 31). *First trimester problems: When to call your doctor.* WebMD. https://www.webmd.com/baby/features/pregnancy-first-trimester-warning-signs

Marple, K. (2021, July 19). *3 weeks pregnant.* BabyCenter. https://www.babycenter.com/pregnancy/week-by-week/3-weeks-pregnant

Marple, K. (2022a, March 15). *9 weeks pregnant.* BabyCenter. https://www.babycenter.com/pregnancy/week-by-week/9-weeks-pregnant

Marple, K. (2022b, March 15). *10 weeks pregnant.* BabyCenter. https://www.babycenter.com/pregnancy/week-by-week/10-weeks-pregnant

Masters, M. (2020, July 9). *5 things every partner should do for a mom-to-be.* What to Expect. https://www.whattoexpect.com/pregnancy/for-dad/pregnancy-pointers-for-soon-to-be-dads.aspx

Montgomery, S. (2017, July 18). *8 ways my partner made me feel confident during pregnancy.* Romper. https://www.romper.com/p/8-ways-my-partner-made-me-feel-confident-during-pregnancy-70653

Murphy, H. (2019, June 7). *9 ways every grown-ass man helps with morning sickness.* Romper. https://www.romper.com/p/9-ways-every-grown-ass-man-helps-with-morning-sickness-11884

Paolelli, M. (2019, December 20). *6 ways to help ease your partner's morning sickness—Motherly*. Motherly. https://www.mother.ly/preg nancy/first-trimester/morning-sickness6-ways-partner-can-help/

Pevzner, H. (2021a, June 14). *Week 2 of your pregnancy*. Verywell Family. https://www.verywellfamily.com/2-weeks-pregnant-4158819

Pevzner, H. (2021b, June 14). *Week 11 of your pregnancy*. Verywell Family. https://www.verywellfamily.com/11-weeks-pregnant-4158930

Pevzner, H. (2021c, June 14). *Week 14 of your pregnancy*. Verywell Family. https://www.verywellfamily.com/14-weeks-pregnant-4158944

Pevzner, H. (2021d, July 19). *Week 5 of your pregnancy*. Verywell Family. https://www.verywellfamily.com/5-weeks-pregnant-4158868

Sinrich, J. (2021, May 7). *4 ways to save for your baby's future*. What to Expect. https://www.whattoexpect.com/pregnancy/save-for-your-babys-future.aspx

Smith, R. (2019, November 20). *Saving up for baby*. TheBUMP. https://www.thebump.com/a/advice-for-saving-up-for-a-baby

Wahlberg, R. (2021, October 6). *Is it safe to change cat litter during pregnancy?* BabyCenter. https://www.babycenter.com/pregnancy/health-and-safety/is-it-safe-to-change-the-cats-litter-box-when-im-pregnant_1246885

Weiss, R. E. (2021, September 13). *Don't offend your partner when she says she's pregnant*. Verywell Family. https://www.verywellfamily.com/what-not-to-say-when-your-partner-says-shes-pregnant-4111036

Printed in Poland
by Amazon Fulfillment
Poland Sp. z o.o., Wrocław
30 November 2022

3e203f17-2c47-48fc-ac26-d74cc26f2217R01